Cupcake Handbook

Your Guide to More Than 80 Recipes for Every Occasion

Sue McMahon

IMM **lifestyle**
books™
Read. Learn. Do What You Love.

To my mother, Peggy McMahon, who has always encouraged me to make
and decorate cakes from when I was very young. She has shared her
love and enthusiasm of baking with me, and I hope that readers
of this book will now enjoy sharing those skills.

Published 2018—IMM Lifestyle Books
www.IMMLifestyleBooks.com

IMM Lifestyle Books are distributed in the UK by Grantham Book Service, Trent Road,
Grantham, Lincolnshire, NG31 7XQ.

In North America, IMM Lifestyle Books are distributed by Fox Chapel Publishing, 903 Square
Street, Mount Joy, PA 17552, www.FoxChapelPublishing.com.

© 2018 by IMM Lifestyle Books

Produced under license.

ISBN 978-1-5048-0092-1

The Cataloging-in-Publication Data is on file with the Library of Congress.

We are always looking for talented authors. To submit an idea, please send a brief inquiry to
acquisitions@foxchapelpublishing.com.

Printed in China
10 9 8 7 6 5 4 3 2 1

This book has been published with the intent to provide accurate and authoritative information
in regard to the subject matter within. While every precaution has been taken in the
preparation of this book, the author and publisher expressly disclaim any responsibility for
any errors, omissions, or adverse effects arising from the use or application of the information
contained herein.

Contents

Introduction

· · · · · · · · ·

Cupcakes are just about perfect for an afternoon treat or a stunning centerpiece at an elaborate wedding—everybody has his or her own "mini" cake, and no one argues over who gets the biggest slice! Besides their convenience, cupcakes are long lasting, too. Baking the cupcakes in liners seals the sides, and if the tops are iced completely, then the cakes are totally sealed and will stay fresh until they're ready for your occasion, big or small.

Baking

Position the oven shelf slightly below the center of the oven so the cakes sit in the center of the oven. It is possible to cook two trays of cupcakes at the same time if you double the recipe ingredients, but allow an extra 5 minutes' cooking time and swap the position of the trays in the oven after 10 to 12 minutes so that both trays cook evenly.

Serving

If the cupcakes are topped with a soft frosting, don't stack them directly on top of one another because the frosting will be ruined. Instead, use a tiered stand to display the cakes. You should have no trouble finding stands made specifically for holding regular-size cupcakes!

Storing

Store cupcakes in an airtight container to keep them fresh. Unless they contain fresh cream, cupcakes shouldn't be refrigerated (except if the room is very warm), since chilling tends to dry them out. Keep the cakes out of bright sunlight to keep the frosting from melting.

Freezing

Basic cupcakes may be made in advance and then frozen—without the frosting. Use thicker cupcake liners, such as foil ones, since thinner liners will wrinkle during freezing and will peel away from the cupcakes. Allow the cupcakes to defrost thoroughly in a cool place for 4 to 6 hours before frosting.

GETTING READY

Equipment

· · · · · · · · · ·

There are two basic items you need in order to make cupcakes—
muffin/cupcake pans and cupcake liners—but they need to match up.
The liners must fit snugly inside the cups of the pan, and the pan must
support the cupcakes during cooking so they hold their shape. Make
sure the cupcake liners you use aren't smaller than the cups in your
pan or you'll find that the sides of the liners will open during
baking and you'll be left with flat cupcakes. The recipes in
this book are based on standard-size muffin/cupcake pans,
but if your trays are larger, just make fewer cakes.

Muffin/Cupcake pans

The best type of muffin/cupcake pans are metal ones, since metal conducts heat well, allowing the cupcakes to cook quickly and evenly. If you choose pans with a nonstick coating, they will be easier to clean if any of the cake mixture overflows during baking. Many of the nonstick pans are dishwasher safe. Whichever type you choose, make sure the pan is spotlessly clean before using and dry thoroughly after use so that it doesn't rust. Ceramic pans and silicone molds are also available, but cupcakes will take slightly longer to cook in these since the materials don't conduct heat as well as metal. All the cupcakes in this book are baked in paper liners; if you use silicone molds, then liners aren't required because the cakes will come easily out of the molds, with smooth sides and hardly any crumbs.

Alternatively, you can buy disposable individual cupcake liners that come with a second outer liner of aluminum foil. This allows you to make as many cupcakes as you want (adjusting your recipe accordingly). With these, all you need is a flat baking sheet.

Paper cupcake liners

Choose good-quality cupcake liners because cheaper, thinner liners can wrinkle during baking. Also, if the liners are made from thin paper, any designs printed on them won't show up well when the cupcakes are baked.

Scales

While the rest of the world measures ingredients by weight, the United States measures by volume. For baking, especially, that can be a problem, since the actual amount of flour or sugar you measure in a cup can change depending on how dense you tamp it or how vigorously you scoop it. Therefore, if you want your cupcakes to come out reliably beautiful and delicious every time, the only truly accurate way to measure ingredients is by using a scale. But make sure you stick to one set of measures—metric or imperial—and avoid mixing the two.

Wire racks

It's important to transfer the cupcakes to a wire rack to cool because if they are left in the muffin/cupcake pans after baking they will steam, and the bottoms of the cupcake liners may get soggy.

Piping bags

It is possible to buy reusable piping bags, such as ones made from cloth, but the easiest type to use are plastic disposable ones, since they don't need to be cleaned afterward. Disposable piping bags are made from a thick plastic, and cutting off the tip will give you a good, strong hole for piping plain lines without the need to use a piping tip.

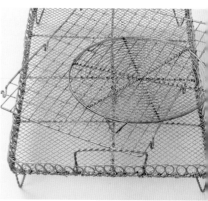

Piping tips

The best piping tips for fine piping are the seamless stainless steel tips. Larger piping tips are best for swirls of icing. Keep the tips in a separate box from the rest of your kitchen utensils so they don't get damaged.

Zesting and juicing

A number of recipes call for the juice and zest of citrus fruits, namely oranges, lemons, and limes. Having a zester and a juicer (a hand juicer works just fine) in your kitchen stash will make these recipes easier—and more fun—to make.

Measuring tools

A basic set of these tools is essential. Make sure you have ¼, ⅓, ½, and 1 cup measures, as well as a teaspoon, tablespoon, and ½ tablespoon. They should be flat rimmed. Either plastic or stainless steel is fine, as long as you keep them clean.

Electric mixer

This tool is a major helper when it comes to making cupcake batter. It will really save your arm when you go to make creams or meringues, and if you're using table sugar instead of superfine sugar this will make your recipes much more successful. Just make sure you

have one that has both beater and paddle extensions.

Blender or food processor

For chopping nuts, fruits, or for converting table sugar into superfine sugar, a blender or food processor comes in extremely handy.

Miscellaneous

- Mortar and pestle, for crushing herbs
- Sieve, for straining jams
- Fine strainer, for topping with confectioners' sugar
- Fondant mat or cutting board and sugar paste/fondant tools
- Parchment paper
- Knife, for slicing fruit and veining sugar paste/fondant leaves

Ingredients

· · · · · · · · ·

Butter

Butter has been recommended throughout this book except where recipes call specifically for oil. If you use margarine or dairy-free butter, make sure it is suitable for baking. In recognition of healthy eating trends, many manufacturers have reduced the fat content of margarines and other spreads. But this means they don't work as well for baking, so either choose butter or a substitute with a fat content of at least 70 percent, and preferably about 80 percent.

Most recipes call for softened butter. There are several ways to soften butter, but the easiest is to set it out in advance and let it reach room temperature. If you're short on time, however, you can set the butter in a mini pot and set the pot in a pan of hot water. Try to avoid using a microwave—the butter will remain hard in some places but melt in others.

How to measure

Butter is measured by sticks (4 oz./ 113 g), ounces (4 ounces per stick), tablespoons (8 tablespoons per stick), and cups (½ cup per stick). So recipes that call for 9 Tbsp. of butter require a full stick of butter (8 Tbsp.) plus a single tablespoon off a new stick.

Sugar

Don't worry too much if you don't have the exact sugar stated in the recipe. You can interchange the fine white sugar, light brown sugar, and dark brown sugar, but if you use the brown sugars you'll find that your cupcakes will have a more molasses-like flavor as well as producing darker cakes.

The difference between superfine (aka extra fine or ultrafine) sugar and granulated (aka table) sugar, in baking, lies chiefly in the mixing of the sugar and the butter. Superfine sugar consists of smaller grains and therefore dissolves faster. That means it's easier and takes less time to beat the butter and sugar to a light and fluffy consistency. Especially if

you're baking with only a hand whisk or fork, using superfine sugar will save you a lot of work. In addition, superfine sugar gives you silkier, smoother cupcakes.

However, superfine sugar—known as "caster sugar" in the United Kingdom and elsewhere—can be more difficult to find at stores than table sugar. Moreover, it's often sold in containers intended for use with beverages, and these are not very big.

In a pinch, a simple workaround is to make your own batch of superfine sugar by pulsing table sugar in a blender or food processor for up to a minute or longer. To avoid confusing it with your regular sugar, make sure you label and store it separately.

13

Confectioners' sugar (or powdered sugar) is used to give toppings a smooth, velvety finish.

Flour

Most recipes call for self-rising flour, which is essential for getting light, fluffy cupcakes. Your local grocery store will likely have name-brand options in stock. Don't make a straight substitute with all-purpose flour—your cupcakes will come out shallow and dense. It's easy to make your own, using the following ratio (multiply proportionately if you need more):

- 1 cup all-purpose flour
- 1½ teaspoons baking powder
- ½ teaspoon table salt

Mix the ingredients and use right away.

Measuring self-rising flour
The best method is to use a scale. But if using cups, for recipes calling for 1 cup (125 g, or 4½ oz.), spoon the flour into a measuring cup and allow it to round or overfill slightly.

Eggs

All eggs used are medium size, unless otherwise stated. Ensure that the eggs are as fresh as possible and use them at room temperature. Avoid eating raw dough containing eggs, as there is a chance of developing a foodborne illness.

Many recipes call for **egg whites**. To separate egg whites from yolks, set out 2 bowls: one for yolks, one for whites. Then follow these steps:

buy colored paste, you can color it yourself using coloring. The easiest way to color a batch of sugar paste/fondant is to break off a small piece and add food coloring until the color is very bold, then knead this piece into the larger piece. The color will work in more easily if it's done in two stages rather than trying to color all of the paste at one time.

Sprinkles

There's a world of edible sprinkle options available in baking aisles and specialty stores, in many different colors, sizes, and shapes—even metallic glitters. Be sure to store them in a dry place and out of bright sunlight, or they will fade.

1. Crack an egg and hold it over the egg whites bowl.
2. Catch the yolk in your hand and let the white run through your fingers into the egg whites bowl.
3. Put the yolk in the yolk bowl.

Alternatively, you can use the shell halves to cup the yolk, transferring it back and forth from shell to shell, while draining off the white.

Note: Recipes that call for raw egg whites to be used as glazing should be avoided by people having high susceptibility to food-borne pathogens.

Sugar paste/fondant

Use store-bought sugar paste/fondant, available from craft or grocery stores. If you're unable to

Veganize it

Vegan cupcakes—made without dairy or eggs—are part of the culture now; almost every little bakery seems to have at least a portion of display case space set aside for vegan customers. And with the prevalence of high-quality vegan ingredients available, making your own at home poses no problems.

Just follow this chart to fully veganize any recipe in this book (any ingredient not listed in the table is already vegan). Keep in mind that some recipes are easier to veganize than others, depending on which ingredients are called for.

Original	Vegan Substitute
butter	vegan butter sticks, such as Earth Balance Vegan Buttery Sticks
eggs	egg replacer, such as Ener-G Egg Replacer. Alternatively, use arrowroot powder (2 Tbsp. for 1 egg), widely available at supermarkets
milk	plain soy, rice, oat, flax, or almond milk
egg whites	egg replacer, such as Ener-G Egg Replacer. Alternatively, use arrowroot powder (2 Tbsp. for 1 egg)
heavy whipping cream	coconut cream (the creamy part in a can of coconut milk; 1:1 substitution). Alternatively, use blended silken tofu for a milder tasting, low-fat option
sweetened condensed milk	simmer and whisk soy milk in a saucepan, adding sugar, until it boils down to a thick, gooey consistency (2½ cups condenses to about 1 cup after about 2 hours)

Original	Vegan Substitute
chocolate (bars, chips, melting wafers)	dark chocolate (any bar that does not list milk as an ingredient)
lemon curd	zest and juice of 1 lemon (to taste) plus 1 cup filler (soy, rice, oat, or almond milk; alternatively, coconut cream or silken tofu) plus ½ cup sweetener (maple syrup, superfine sugar, or agave nectar) plus 4 Tbsp. thickener (corn starch, vegan butter, or arrowroot powder), blended together
sour cream	vegan sour cream, widely available at supermarkets
cream cheese	vegan cream cheese, widely available at supermarkets
digestive biscuits	vegan cookies (vanilla wafers, for instance)
crème fraiche	Use a 1:1 ratio of soy yogurt or soy sour cream with soy cream cheese. Alternatively, blend together one package of silken tofu, ¼ cup nutritional yeast, and a small amount of sweetener
marshmallows	vegan marshmallows, widely available at supermarkets
sugar paste/ fondant	any fondant or fondant mix that does not contain gelatin (check ingredients lists)

BASIC
RECIPES

Plain cupcakes

• • • • • • • •

This recipe provides the basis for many of the decorated cupcakes you'll find in this book.

Makes 12 standard-size cupcakes or 18 to 24 mini cupcakes

- 9 Tbsp. (125 g, or 4½ oz.) butter, softened
- ½ cup (125 g, or 4½ oz.) superfine sugar
- 2 medium eggs
- 1 cup (125 g, or 4½ oz.) self-rising flour
- 2½ Tbsp. milk

1. Preheat oven to 375°F/190°C (gas 5).

2. Beat together the butter and sugar in a bowl until light and fluffy. Add the eggs, flour, and milk to the bowl and beat until the mixture is smooth. Divide the mixture among the cupcake liners and bake in the center of the oven until the cakes have risen and are just firm to the touch in the center. Standard-size cupcakes will take about 12 to 15 minutes and mini cakes about 10 to 12 minutes.

3. Remove the cupcakes from the oven and transfer them to a wire rack to cool.

Chocolate cupcakes

Chocolate cupcakes are always a popular choice for children—but adults will enjoy these, too!

Makes 12 standard-size cupcakes or 18 to 24 mini cupcakes

- 9 Tbsp. (125 g, or 4½ oz.) butter, softened
- ½ cup (125 g, or 4½ oz.) superfine sugar
- 2 medium eggs
- 2½ Tbsp. milk
- ¾ cup plus 1 Tbsp. (100 g, or 3½ oz.) self-rising flour
- 3½ level Tbsp. cocoa

1. Preheat oven to 375°F/190°C (gas 5).

2. Beat together the butter and sugar in a bowl until light and fluffy. Add the eggs and milk.

3. In another bowl, sift the flour and cocoa and then add to the butter mixture. Beat well until smooth.

4. Divide the mixture among the cupcake liners and bake in the center of the oven until the cakes have risen and are just firm to the touch in the center. The standard-size cupcakes will take about 12 to 15 minutes and the mini cakes about 10 to 12 minutes.

5. Remove the cakes from the oven and transfer them to a wire rack to cool.

Lemon cupcakes

• • • • • • • •

The lemon in these cupcakes gives a fresh citrus tang
that goes perfectly with a zingy fruit topping.

Makes 12 standard-size cupcakes
or 18 to 24 mini cupcakes

- 9 Tbsp. (125 g, or 4½ oz.)
  butter, softened
- ½ cup (125 g, or 4½ oz.)
  superfine sugar
- 2 medium eggs
- Finely grated zest and juice
  of 1 lemon
- 1 cup (125 g, or 4½ oz.)
  self-rising flour

1. Preheat oven to 375°F/190°C
   (gas 5).

2. Beat the butter and sugar together
   in a bowl until the mixture is light
   and fluffy. Add the eggs, lemon
   zest, lemon juice, and flour to
   the bowl and beat the mixture
   until smooth.

3. Divide the mixture among the
   cupcake liners and bake in the
   center of the oven until the cakes
   have risen and are just firm to the
   touch in the center. Standard-size
   cupcakes will take about 12 to
   15 minutes and mini cakes about
   10 to 12 minutes.

4. Remove the cakes from the oven
   and transfer them to a wire rack
   to cool.

Quick-mix cupcakes

These cupcakes are quick to mix since no creaming stage is required.
They will have a muffin-like texture.

1. Preheat oven to 400°F/200°C (gas 6).

2. Sift the flour and baking powder into a bowl and stir in the sugar.

3. In a separate bowl, lightly beat together the milk, egg, and oil and stir into the dry ingredients. Stir lightly and don't over-mix or the cakes will be tough.

4. Divide the mixture among the cupcake liners and bake in the center of the oven until the cupcakes are a light golden color and spring back when lightly pressed. Standard-size cakes will take about 12 to 15 minutes and mini cakes about 10 to 12 minutes.

5. Remove the cupcakes from the oven and transfer them to a wire rack to cool.

Makes 12 standard-size cupcakes or 24 mini cupcakes

- 1⅓ cups (175 g, or 6 oz.) self-rising flour
- ½ level tsp. baking powder
- ⅓ cup (75 g, or 2½ oz.) superfine sugar
- ⅔ cup (150 mL, or 5 fl. oz.) milk
- 1 medium egg
- 2½ Tbsp. vegetable oil

Go dairy-free!
Use soy milk instead
of cow's milk.

Vanilla buttercream

This buttercream frosting is quick to make
since no cooking time is required.

*Makes enough for 12 standard-size
cupcakes or 24 mini cupcakes*

- 12 Tbsp. (175 g, or 6 oz.)
  butter, softened
- 2¾ cups (350 g, or 12½ oz.)
  confectioners' sugar
- 3½ Tbsp. boiling water
- Few drops of vanilla extract

1. Beat the butter in a bowl to a
   creamy consistency.

2. Add the sugar, water, and vanilla,
   and beat until the icing is very
   smooth and pale in color.

This buttercream is best
made just before it's going to
be used. If you are making it in
advance, press a sheet of plastic
wrap against the surface of the
frosting and cover the bowl with
a damp cloth to prevent the
frosting from crusting. Beat it
well just before using.

Chocolate buttercream

· · · · · · · · ·

Adding vanilla to this chocolate buttercream frosting
enhances the chocolate flavor.

1. Beat the butter in a bowl to a
   creamy consistency.

2. In a separate bowl, mix the cocoa
   and boiling water to a paste.

3. Add the chocolate mixture to
   the butter and then add the
   confectioners' sugar and vanilla
   and beat until the frosting is
   very smooth.

*Makes enough for 12 standard-size
cupcakes or 24 mini cupcakes*

- 12 Tbsp. (175 g, or 6 oz.)
  butter, softened
- 5 level Tbsp. cocoa
- 3½ Tbsp. boiling water
- 2¾ cups (350 g, or 12½ oz.)
  confectioners' sugar
- Few drops of vanilla extract

As with the Vanilla
buttercream, this frosting is
best made just before it's used. If
you are making it in advance, press
a sheet of plastic wrap against the
surface of the frosting and cover
the bowl with a damp cloth to
prevent the frosting from crusting.
Beat it well just before using.

BASIC RECIPES

Swiss meringue buttercream

Because the sugar is dissolved in the warm egg whites,
this makes an exceptionally smooth buttercream.

Makes enough for 12 standard-size cupcakes or 24 mini cupcakes

- 4 medium egg whites
- 1 cup plus 1 Tbsp. (250 g, or 9 oz.) superfine sugar
- Pinch of salt
- 17 Tbsp. (250 g, 9 oz.) unsalted butter, softened
- Few drops of vanilla extract

This buttercream is stable for 1 to 2 days at room temperature (no higher than 59°F (15°C); otherwise, it may be refrigerated for up to 2 weeks.

1. Place the egg whites, sugar, and salt in a bowl over a pan of simmering water and mix together well. Stir frequently while heating to prevent the egg whites from cooking.

2. After about 5 to 10 minutes, when the mixture is warm and the sugar crystals have dissolved, remove the bowl from the heat. Whisk the meringue to full volume until the mixture is cool.

3. Add the butter and vanilla to the meringue—the mixture will reduce in volume and appear curdled. Continue to whisk until the butter emulsifies completely into the meringue and forms a smooth, light, and fluffy texture.

Lemon cream cheese frosting

This basic recipe may be altered by using orange or lime in place of lemon.

Makes enough for 12 standard-size cupcakes or 24 mini cupcakes

- 10½ oz. (300 g) cream cheese
- Finely grated zest and juice of 1 lemon
- 3½–5 Tbsp. confectioners' sugar

1. Beat the cream cheese to soften it, then beat in the lemon zest and juice.

2. Beat in confectioners' sugar to taste.

Use full-fat cream cheese rather than lowfat cheeses, which are usually softer and may result in a frosting that is too runny.

Chocolate ganache

* * * * * * * * *

This rich and smooth ganache is best made
with a very dark chocolate.

*Makes enough for 12 standard-size
cupcakes or 24 mini cupcakes*

- 1¼ cups (284 mL, or 9½
  fl. oz.) heavy whipping cream
- 1 level Tbsp. light corn syrup
- 7 oz. (200 g) dark chocolate,
  coarsely chopped

1. Bring the cream to a boil in a
   saucepan, then remove the pan
   from the heat and stir in the light
   corn syrup.

2. Place the chocolate in a bowl
   and pour the cream over the
   chocolate. Stir until the chocolate
   melts completely and the ganache
   is smooth.

Ganache may be used warm
after it has thickened slightly and
is of a pouring consistency or it
may be left until it's cool enough to
be of a coating consistency to give a
glossy topping. Use a palette knife
to spread it. Alternatively, it may
be left to cool completely and then
whisked to give a lighter texture.
If it thickens too much, it can
be gently warmed.

Royal icing

This recipe produces a royal icing that has a smooth, stiff consistency. It dries hard, making it ideal for creating decorations like the piped flowers on the Spring garden cupcakes on page 154. To use as a softer icing for covering cupcakes, add approximately 1 tablespoon of glycerine to every 3 cups (350 g, or 12½ oz.) of icing.

Makes enough for 12 standard-size cupcakes or 24 mini cupcakes

- ° 2 large egg whites
- ° 2¾–4 cups (350–500 g, or 2½–18 oz.) confectioners' sugar

Royal icing will keep for up to two days. Press a sheet of plastic wrap against the surface and cover the bowl with a damp cloth. Store in a cool place but do not refrigerate, and ensure the cloth remains damp.

1. Using an electric mixer, lightly beat the egg whites to break them down.

2. Using the paddle beater rather than a whisk, gradually beat in the confectioners' sugar. Add enough confectioners' sugar until the mixture starts to thicken, then beat using the lowest speed for about 10 minutes, until the icing is light and fluffy.

3. Adjust the consistency if necessary by either adding more confectioners' sugar if the mixture is too runny, or a few drops of water if it's too stiff—but beat for at least 2 to 3 minutes after each addition of confectioners' sugar.

Thick glacé icing

This versatile icing can be used on almost any cupcake. Add more or less water to achieve different consistencies.

Makes enough for 12 standard-size cupcakes or 24 mini cupcakes

- 2–2¾ cups (250–350 g, or 9–12½ oz.) confectioners' sugar
- 2½–5 Tbsp. water
- Liquid or paste food coloring

1. Sift the confectioners' sugar into a bowl and gradually beat in the water, 1 tablespoon at a time, to give a thick, smooth, glossy icing.

2. Add the food coloring gradually until you have achieved the desired color.

3. Make the icing a few minutes before it is needed. Stir the icing regularly and place a sheet of plastic wrap on the surface and keep the bowl covered with a damp cloth to prevent the icing from crusting over.

Liquid food coloring should be added drop by drop. Paste coloring should also be added in very small quantities, using the tip of a knife.

Satin icing

• • • • • • • •

This is a thick icing that will set with a satin-like sheen. It should be used as soon as it is made, since it crusts over very quickly and needs to be spread over the cupcakes while it's still warm.

Makes enough for 12 standard-size cupcakes or 24 mini cupcakes

- ° ¼ cup (45 g, or 1½ oz.) vegetable shortening
- ° 5 Tbsp. lemon juice
- ° 2¾ cups (350 g, or 12½ oz.) confectioners' sugar
- ° Liquid food coloring (optional)
- ° 1–2½ Tbsp. hot water

1. Melt the shortening in a large saucepan over low heat. Remove the pan from the heat and stir in the lemon juice and half of the confectioners' sugar. Beat the mixture well. Return the pan to the heat and simmer for about 1 minute until bubbles appear all over the surface.

2. When bubbles start to form, immediately remove the pan from the heat. Beat in the remaining confectioners' sugar, food coloring, if using, and sufficient hot water to give a thick pouring consistency. Beat well to remove any lumps and use the icing immediately before it starts to cool and set.

3. Spoon the icing over the cupcakes, working quickly and spreading the icing if necessary with a palette knife dipped in hot water to give a smooth surface.

Toffee topping

Using condensed milk in this recipe gives a really rich, creamy toffee.
Use this topping while it's hot on other desserts, too!

1. Place the butter in a large bowl and melt it in the microwave for about 30 to 40 seconds. Stir in the condensed milk, sugar, and golden syrup.

2. Cook the topping in the microwave for 4 to 7 minutes on high power, stirring it at the end of every minute until it is a pale golden color. (Alternatively, the topping can be cooked in a saucepan for 4 to 7 minutes, stirring continuously so that it does not stick to the base of the pan.)

3. Let the topping cool and thicken slightly, then spread over the cupcakes using a palette knife.

The topping may be made up to two days in advance and kept refrigerated. Warm it through gently until it is smooth before using.

Makes enough for 12 standard-size cupcakes or 24 mini cupcakes

- 7 Tbsp. (100 g, or 3½ oz.) butter
- ⅓ cup (125 g, or 4½ oz.) sweetened condensed milk
- ¼ cup (50 g, or 2 oz.) superfine sugar
- 1 Tbsp. golden syrup*

*Look in the international or baking aisle of your local supermarket for this English baking syrup. If you have trouble finding it, you can either order it online or substitute (see page 188).

Modeling chocolate

· · · · · · · ·

This molding chocolate can be rolled out like sugar paste/fondant
for covering cupcakes or making molded decorations
like flowers or animals.

*Makes enough for 12 roses and
36 leaves*

- ½ cup (150 g, or 5½ oz.)
  golden syrup*
- 10½ oz. (300 g)
  chocolate, melted
- Cocoa, for dusting

* See page 188

This recipe uses regular
chocolate, but for white
modeling chocolate use white
chocolate and if it's sticky, use
a little confectioners' sugar
instead of cocoa.

1. Stir the golden syrup into the
   melted chocolate, until the mixture
   thickens. It may look as if it has
   separated, but on chilling it will
   form a smooth paste. Transfer the
   mixture to a plastic bag and chill
   until the chocolate is firm enough
   to handle.

2. Knead the modeling chocolate
   lightly to soften it before using.
   If it's sticky, use cocoa to keep it
   from sticking.

3. If your hands are hot, run
   them under cold water to cool
   them before working with the
   modeling chocolate.

CLASSIC
COMBINATIONS

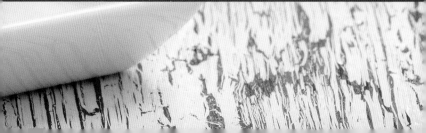

Banana and toffee

For best flavor, use a ripe or overripe banana.

Makes 12 standard-size cupcakes

For the cupcakes

- 7 Tbsp. (100 g, or 3½ oz.) butter, softened
- ½ cup (100 g, or 3½ oz.) light brown sugar
- 2 medium eggs
- ¾ cup plus 1 Tbsp. (100 g, or 3½ oz.) self-rising flour
- 1 ripe banana, mashed

For the topping

- 1 quantity of Toffee topping, see page 39
- 3½–5 Tbsp. chocolate chips

1. Preheat the oven to 375°F/190°C (gas 5).

2. To make the cupcakes, beat the butter and sugar together in a bowl until the mixture is light and fluffy.

3. Add the eggs and flour to the bowl. Beat until the mixture is smooth, then fold in the banana.

4. Divide the mixture among the cupcake liners and bake in the center of the oven for 12 to 15 minutes until the cakes have risen and are just firm to the touch in the center. Remove the cakes from the oven and transfer them to a wire rack to cool.

5. Spread toffee topping over each cupcake and decorate with the chocolate chips.

Mint chocolate chip

. . . .

Coloring the cupcakes green makes them look slightly unusual, but they look great with the topping!

Makes 12 standard-size cupcakes

For the cupcakes

- 9 Tbsp. (125 g, or 4½ oz.) butter, softened
- ½ cup (125 g, or 4½ oz.) superfine sugar
- 2 medium eggs
- 1 cup (125g, or 4½ oz.) self-rising flour
- Few drops of peppermint flavoring
- Few drops of green food coloring
- 3½ oz. (100 g) chocolate chips

For the topping

- 1 quantity of Vanilla buttercream, see page 26
- Few drops of green food coloring
- Few drops of peppermint flavoring
- 3–5 Tbsp. chocolate sprinkles

1. Preheat the oven to 375°F/190°C (gas 5).

2. To make the cupcakes, beat the butter and sugar together in a bowl until the mixture is light and fluffy.

3. Add the eggs, flour, peppermint flavoring, and green food coloring, and beat the mixture until smooth. Then stir in the chocolate chips.

4. Divide the mixture among the cupcake liners and bake in the center of the oven for 12 to 15 minutes until the cupcakes have risen and are just firm to the touch in the center. Remove the cupcakes from the oven and transfer them to a wire rack to cool.

5. For the topping, add some green coloring to the buttercream, and flavor to taste with the peppermint. Spread the buttercream over the cupcakes, and decorate with the chocolate sprinkles.

Coffee and walnut

Topped with a coffee buttercream and walnuts,
these cupcakes will delight mocha lovers.

Makes 12 standard-size cupcakes

For the cupcakes

- 1¼ cups (150 g, or 5½ oz.)
  self-rising flour
- ½ cup (60 g, or 2 oz.)
  walnuts
- 11 Tbsp. (150 g, or 5½ oz.)
  butter, softened
- ¾ cup (150 g, or 5½ oz.)
  light brown sugar
- 3 medium eggs
- 2½ Tbsp. instant
  coffee granules
- 1½ Tbsp. boiling water

For the topping

- 1 Tbsp. instant coffee granules
- 1 Tbsp. boiling water
- 6 Tbsp. (90 g, or 3 oz.)
  butter, softened
- 1½ cups (175 g, or 6 oz.)
  confectioners' sugar
- 12 walnut halves
- Confectioners' sugar
  for dusting

1. Preheat the oven to 375°F/190°C
   (gas 5).

2. To make the cupcakes, pour the
   flour and walnuts into the bowl of
   a food processor and pulse until
   the nuts are finely ground.

3. Beat the butter and sugar in a bowl
   until the mixture is light and fluffy,
   then add the eggs, then the flour
   and walnut mixture.

4. Pour the coffee granules into
   a small bowl, add the boiling
   water, and stir until the coffee has
   dissolved. Then add to the cake
   ingredients in the bowl, beating the
   mixture until smooth.

5. Divide the mixture among the
   cupcake liners and bake in the
   center of the oven for 15 to
   20 minutes until the cakes have
   risen and are just firm to the touch
   in the center. Remove the cakes
   from the oven and transfer them to
   a wire rack to cool.

6. To make the topping, pour the coffee granules into a mixing bowl, add the boiling water, and stir until the coffee has dissolved. Add the butter to the bowl and beat until smooth, then gradually beat in the sugar until fluffy. Spread the icing over the tops of the cupcakes and place a walnut half on top of each. Dust with confectioners' sugar before serving.

Strawberries 'n' cream

These cupcakes taste best topped with fresh cream, but if it's warm and you don't think the fresh cream will last, you can substitute the Swiss meringue buttercream (page 28).

Makes 12 standard-size cupcakes

For the cupcakes

- 12 standard-size Plain cupcakes, see page 20
- 7 Tbsp. strawberry jam

For the topping

- 1 cup plus 3 Tbsp. (284 mL, or 9½ fl. oz.) heavy whipping cream
- 2½ Tbsp. confectioners' sugar
- 6 medium strawberries, halved

1. Cut the top off each cupcake and reserve the tops for "lids." Spread the cut surface with the jam, then replace the lids.

2. For the topping, pour the cream into a bowl and add the sugar. Lightly whip the cream until it forms soft peaks, then spoon onto the top of each cupcake. Finish by pressing half a strawberry on top. Keep the cupcakes chilled until ready for serving.

Apple and cinnamon

The apple slices look best with the skin left on,
particularly if you use red-skinned apples.

Makes 12 standard-size cupcakes

For the cupcakes

- 9 Tbsp. (125 g, or 4½ oz.) butter, softened
- ⅔ cup (125 g, or 4½ oz.) light brown sugar
- 2 medium eggs
- 1 cup (125 g, or 4½ oz.) self-rising flour
- 2½ level tsp. ground cinnamon
- 1 apple, cored and grated
- 1 apple, cored and sliced

For the topping

- 5–7 Tbsp. apricot glaze or apricot jam, strained through a sieve
- 2½ Tbsp. water

1. Preheat the oven to 375°F/190°C (gas 5).

2. To make the cakes, beat together the butter and sugar in a bowl until the mixture is light and fluffy. Add the eggs and then sift the flour and cinnamon together into the bowl. Beat the mixture until smooth, then stir in the grated apple.

3. Divide the mixture among the cupcake liners and arrange the apple slices on top of the cakes. Bake in the center of the oven for 12 to 15 minutes until the cakes have risen and are just firm to the touch in the center. Remove the cakes from the oven and transfer them to a wire rack.

4. For the topping, warm the apricot glaze or jam with the water and combine, either in a saucepan or in a microwave. Then brush the jam over the tops of the hot cupcakes. Serve warm or cool.

Double chocolate

Both plain and white chocolate are used in these cupcakes,
giving them a rich chocolate flavor.

Makes 12 standard-size cupcakes

For the cupcakes

- 9 Tbsp. (125 g, or 4½ oz.) butter, softened
- ½ cup (125 g, or 4½ oz.) superfine sugar
- 2 medium eggs
- ¾ cup (90 g, or 3 oz.) self-rising flour
- ⅓ cup (30 g, or 1 oz.) cocoa
- 3½ oz. (100 g) white chocolate chips

For the topping

- 1 quantity of Chocolate ganache, see page 32
- 60 white chocolate melting wafers

1. Preheat the oven to 375°F/190°C (gas 5).

2. To make the cupcakes, beat the butter and sugar together until the mixture is light and fluffy. Add the eggs to the bowl, then sift in the flour and cocoa. Beat the mixture until smooth. Stir in the chocolate chips.

3. Divide the mixture among the cupcake liners and bake in the center of the oven for 12 to 15 minutes until the cakes have risen and are just firm to the touch in the center. Remove the cakes from the oven and transfer them to a wire rack to cool.

4. For the topping, spread the ganache over the top of the cupcakes and decorate each cake with five white chocolate wafers.

Black forest

• • • • • • • •

These cupcakes are based on the classic cake recipe that originated in the Black Forest region of Germany.

Makes 12 standard-size cupcakes

For the syrup

- ⅔ cup (150 mL, or 5 fl. oz.) water
- ¼ cup (60 g, or 2 oz.) superfine sugar
- 3½ Tbsp. kirsch

For the cupcakes

- 12 Chocolate cupcakes, see page 22
- 7 level Tbsp. black cherry conserve

For the topping

- 1¼ cups (284 mL, or 9½ fl. oz.) heavy whipping cream
- 12 fresh cherries with stems
- 1–2½ Tbsp. grated chocolate
- Piping bag fitted with large star piping tip

1. To make the syrup, pour the water into a saucepan and add the sugar. Place the pan over low heat and stir until the sugar has dissolved. Increase the heat and boil rapidly until the mixture has reduced by about half. Remove the pan from the heat and allow the syrup to cool for about 5 minutes, then stir in the kirsch.

2. Cut the top off each cupcake and reserve the tops for "lids." Scoop out a small amount of the cake to create a small hollow in each. Brush the warm syrup into the hollows and spoon a little of the black cherry conserve into each hollow, then replace the lids on the cakes.

3. For the topping, whisk the cream until it forms soft peaks, then spoon it into a piping bag fitted with a large star piping tip. Pipe a swirl of cream on top of each cupcake. Place a cherry on top of each and sprinkle each cupcake with a little grated chocolate.

Bakewell

The Derbyshire town of Bakewell in England claims to be where the renowned Bakewell pudding originated, and these cupcakes are a twist on the classic version.

Makes 12 standard-size cupcakes

For the cupcakes

- 9 Tbsp. (125 g, or 4½ oz.) butter, softened
- ½ cup (125 g, or 4½ oz.) superfine sugar
- Few drops of almond extract
- 2 medium eggs
- 2½ Tbsp. milk
- ¾ cup plus 1 Tbsp. (100 g, or 3½ oz.) self-rising flour
- ¼ cup (30 g, or 1 oz.) ground almonds
- 2–3½ Tbsp. sliced almonds

For the topping

- 6–7 Tbsp. raspberry jam
- Confectioners' sugar for dusting

1. Preheat the oven to 375°F/190°C (gas 5).

2. To make the cupcakes, beat the butter, sugar, and almond extract together in a bowl until the mixture is light and fluffy. Add the eggs, milk, flour, and ground almonds and beat until the mixture is smooth.

3. Divide the mixture among the cupcake liners. Scatter the sliced almonds for the topping over the top of each cupcake and press them down slightly into the mixture.

4. Bake in the center of the oven for 12 to 15 minutes until the cupcakes have risen and are just firm to the touch in the center and the almonds are a light golden color. Remove the cakes from the oven and transfer them to a wire rack to cool.

5. Slice the tops off the cakes, spread them with the jam, then replace the tops. Dust with confectioners' sugar before serving.

Carrot and raisin

Decorating these cakes with a sugar carrot makes it clear what flavor they are, but as an alternative, top them with some chopped nuts. These carrots are homemade, but you can use ready-made sugar or marzipan carrots from stores where cake supplies are sold.

Makes 12 standard-size cupcakes

For the cupcakes

- 1¼ cups (150 g, or 5½ oz.) self-rising flour
- ½ tsp. baking powder
- 1 tsp. ground allspice
- ¼ cup (60 g, or 2 oz.) light brown sugar
- 1 carrot, peeled and grated
- ⅓ cup (60 g, or 2 oz.) raisins
- ½ cup (125 mL, or 4¼ fl. oz.) milk
- 1 medium egg
- 2 Tbsp. vegetable oil

For the topping

- 1 quantity of Lemon cream cheese frosting, see page 30
- 12 sugar paste/fondant carrots

1. Preheat the oven to 400°F/200°C (gas 6).

2. To make the cupcakes, sift the flour, baking powder, and allspice into a bowl. Stir in the sugar, carrot, and raisins.

3. In a separate bowl, lightly beat together the milk, egg, and oil, and stir into the flour mixture. Stir lightly and make sure you don't over-mix or the cakes will be tough.

4. Divide the mixture among the cupcake liners and bake in the center of the oven for 15 to 18 minutes until the cakes have risen and are just firm to the touch in the center. Remove the cakes from the oven and transfer them to a wire rack to cool.

5. For the topping, spread the frosting over the cupcakes and decorate each one with a carrot.

Lemon meringue

. . . .

The meringue on the tops of these cakes is an Italian-style meringue, which is smoother than the traditional meringue made from whisked egg whites and sugar.

Makes 12 standard-size cupcakes

For the cupcakes
- 12 Lemon cupcakes, see page 24

For the topping
- 5–7 Tbsp. lemon curd
- Piping bag fitted with star piping tip

For the meringue
- 3½ Tbsp. water
- ¾ cup (175 g, or 6 oz.) superfine sugar
- 1 level Tbsp. light corn syrup
- 3 large egg whites

You can also cook the meringue using a heat gun. Place the cakes on a wooden board to protect the work surface. Hold the heat gun over the meringue until it reaches the desired color.

1. Preheat the oven to 375°F/190°C (gas 5).

2. Spread the lemon curd over the tops of the cupcakes and place them on a baking tray.

3. To make the meringue, pour the water into a small saucepan and add the sugar. Place the pan over medium heat and stir until the sugar has dissolved. Add the light corn syrup to the pan and stir briefly until dissolved. Wash down any sugar crystals on the side of the pan with a damp pastry brush. Increase the heat and boil the mixture rapidly until it reaches 248°F (121°C), occasionally washing down the sides of the pan. Meanwhile whisk the egg whites until stiff. When the sugar has reached the correct temperature, remove the pan from the heat and plunge the base of the pan into a bowl of cold water to stop the cooking process.

62

4. With an electric mixer running at slow speed, gradually pour the syrup over the egg whites. Continue whisking at high speed until the mixture cools. Fill a piping bag fitted with a star piping tip with the meringue mixture and swirl over the lemon curd.

5. Bake the cakes in the center of the oven for 2 to 3 minutes or until the meringue is a light golden color. Remove from the oven and serve immediately or within 2 hours.

Brownies

· · · · · · · ·

To save time and to make these cupcakes less rich, omit the ganache topping and dust the cupcakes with confectioners' sugar instead.

Makes 12 standard-size cupcakes

For the cupcakes

- 3½ oz. (100 g) chocolate
- 9 Tbsp. (125 g, or 4½ oz.) butter, softened
- 2 medium eggs
- ¾ cup (150 g, or 5½ oz.) dark brown sugar
- ½ cup (60 g, or 2 oz.) all-purpose flour
- ¾ cup (100 g, or 3½ oz.) toasted pecans, coarsely chopped

For the topping

- 1 quantity of Chocolate ganache, see page 32
- 12 pecan nuts
- Confectioners' sugar for dusting

1. Preheat the oven to 375°F (190°C).

2. To make the cupcakes, melt the chocolate in a bowl over a pan of hot water. Cool slightly, then whisk the butter into the chocolate.

3. In a separate bowl, lightly whisk the eggs and sugar until the mixture is slightly foamy but not too thick. Fold the egg mixture into the chocolate mixture, and then sift and fold in the flour. Finally fold in the nuts. Divide the mixture among the cupcake liners and bake in the center of the oven for 18 to 20 minutes until the cakes have risen and are just firm to the touch in the center. Remove the cakes from the oven and transfer them to a wire rack to cool.

4. Spread the ganache over the tops of the cupcakes, top with a pecan, and dust with confectioners' sugar.

Blondies

. . . .

A pale version of a brownie, these cupcakes have a butterscotch-like flavor.

Makes 12 standard-size cupcakes

For the cupcakes

- ⅔ cup (125 g, or 4½ oz.) light brown sugar
- 9 Tbsp. (125 g, or 4½ oz.) butter, softened
- 2 medium eggs
- Few drops of vanilla extract
- 1 cup (125 g, or 4½ oz.) self-rising flour

For the topping

- 3½ oz. (100 g) chocolate chips
- 1 cup (125 g, or 4½ oz.) chopped mixed nuts

1. Preheat the oven to 375°F/190°C (gas 5).

2. Heat the sugar and butter in a pan over a gentle heat, stirring until the sugar has dissolved. Remove the pan from the heat and let the mixture cool slightly. Stir in the eggs, one at a time, and then the vanilla extract. Fold in the flour and then divide the mixture among the cupcake liners.

3. For the topping, sprinkle the chocolate chips and nuts on top of each cake, and press lightly into the mixture. Bake in the center of the oven for 18 to 20 minutes until the cakes have risen and are just firm to the touch in the center. Remove the cakes from the oven and transfer them to a wire rack to cool.

Toffee apple

The caramel decorations make these cupcakes special, but if it's humid, they may get cloudy and sticky very quickly, so only decorate the cakes just before serving.

Makes 12 standard-size cupcakes

For the cupcakes
- 6 Tbsp. (90 g, or 3 oz.) butter
- ½ cup (90 g, or 3 oz.) light brown sugar
- 2 medium eggs
- ¾ cup (90 g, or 3 oz.) self-rising flour
- 1 small apple, peeled, cored, and chopped

For the topping and decoration
- ⅓ cup plus 1½ Tbsp. (100 mL, or 3½ fl. oz.) water
- 1½ cups (350 g, or 12½ oz.) superfine sugar
- 2 Tbsp. (30 g, or 1 oz.) butter
- Baking sheet lined with parchment paper

1. Preheat the oven to 375°F/190°C (gas 5).

2. To make the cupcakes, beat the butter and sugar together until the mixture is light and fluffy. Add the eggs and flour and beat until the mixture is smooth. Stir in the chopped apple.

3. Divide the mixture among the cupcake liners and bake in the center of the oven for 12 to 15 minutes until the cakes have risen and are just firm to the touch in the center. Remove the cakes from the oven and transfer them to a wire rack to cool.

4. For the topping and decoration, in a small saucepan combine the water and sugar. Place the pan over gentle heat and stir until the sugar crystals have melted. Use a damp pastry brush to wash down any sugar crystals from the sides of the pan, then increase the heat

and boil the mixture, without stirring, until the sugar turns to a caramel color. Remove the pan from the heat and let the caramel cool slightly. Pour half the caramel into shapes on a baking sheet lined with parchment paper, and let them cool.

5. Gently rewarm the remaining caramel with the butter, and working quickly and on one cupcake at a time, spread some of the butter caramel over the cake, using an oiled palette knife. Make 1 or 2 small holes in the top, then stick in 1 or 2 of the caramel decorations.

69

Baked vanilla cheesecake

* * * * * * * * *

You will find it easier to eat these cupcakes with a small fork or spoon rather than with your fingers.

Makes 12 standard-size cupcakes

For the cupcakes

- ¾ cup (100 g, or 3½ oz.) crushed digestive biscuits or graham crackers
- 2 Tbsp. (30 g, or 1 oz.) butter, melted
- 10½ oz. (300 g) cream cheese
- ¼ cup (60 g, or 2 oz.) superfine sugar
- 2 medium eggs
- Few drops of vanilla extract

For the topping

- ⅔ cup (142 mL, or 5 fl. oz.) sour cream
- 2 Tbsp. (30 g, or 1 oz.) superfine sugar

1. Preheat the oven to 325°F/160°C (gas 3).

2. In a bowl, mix together the crushed biscuits or graham crackers with the butter and divide between the cupcake liners. Press the mixture down firmly.

3. Beat the cream cheese to soften, then beat in the sugar, eggs, and vanilla extract. Divide the mixture among the cupcake liners. Bake in the center of the oven for 15 to 20 minutes, or until the center feels set when pressed lightly.

4. For the topping, mix together the sour cream and sugar, and pour it over the cheesecakes, then return them to the oven for an additional 10 to 15 minutes until the topping has set.

5. Remove the cupcakes from the oven and leave them in the pan to cool. Refrigerate the cheesecakes in the muffin pan, preferably overnight, before serving.

CLASSIC COMBINATIONS

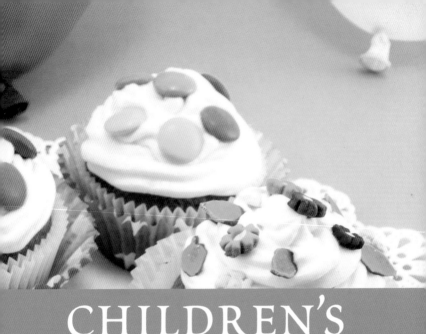

CHILDREN'S FAVORITES

Citrus bursts

These tangy cakes have a refreshing citrus taste. As an alternative, use a lime instead of the orange to make lemon-lime cupcakes.

CHILDREN'S FAVORITES

Makes 12 standard-size cupcakes

For the cupcakes
- 9 Tbsp. (125 g, or 4½ oz.) butter, softened
- ½ cup (125 g, or 4½ oz.) superfine sugar
- 2 medium eggs
- 1 cup (125 g, or 4½ oz.) self-rising flour
- Finely grated zest of 1 lemon and 2½ Tbsp. juice
- Finely grated zest and 2½ Tbsp. juice of 1 orange

For the topping
- 1 quantity of Thick glacé icing, see page 36
- Yellow and orange food coloring
- Small disposable piping bag

1. Preheat the oven to 375°F/190°C (gas 5).

2. To make the cupcakes, beat the butter and sugar in a bowl until the mixture is light and fluffy. Add the eggs, flour, and lemon and orange juices, and beat until smooth. Stir in the lemon and orange zests.

3. Divide the mixture among the cupcake liners and bake in the center of the oven for 12 to 15 minutes until the cakes have risen and are just firm to the touch in the center. Remove the cakes from the oven and transfer them to a wire rack to cool. Cut off the tops of the cakes to level them, if necessary.

4. For the topping, remove about 2 tablespoons of the icing, color it orange, and fill a small, disposable piping bag. Set the piping bag aside. Color the remaining icing yellow and spread some over each cake. Cut off the tip of the icing bag so that you have a small hole, then pipe lines over the orange icing on each cupcake before serving.

Raspberry and white chocolate

These mini cakes are a good way to encourage children to eat fruit!

CHILDREN'S FAVORITES

Makes 24 mini cupcakes

For the cupcakes

- 4 Tbsp. (50 g, or 2 oz.) butter, softened
- ¼ cup (50 g, or 2 oz.) superfine sugar
- 1 medium egg
- ½ cup (50 g, or 2 oz.) self-rising flour
- 1 Tbsp. milk
- 2 oz. (50 g) white chocolate, chopped

For the topping

- ⅓ cup plus 1½ Tbsp. (100 mL, or 3½ fl. oz.) crème fraîche
- 7 oz. (200 g) white chocolate, melted
- 24 raspberries
- Piping bag fitted with large plain piping tip (optional)

1. Preheat the oven to 375°F/190°C (gas 5).

2. To make the cupcakes, beat the butter and sugar together in a bowl until the mixture is light and fluffy. Add the egg, flour, and milk to the bowl and beat until smooth. Fold in the chocolate.

3. Divide the mixture among the cupcake liners in a mini muffin/cupcake pan, and bake in the center of the oven for 12 to 15 minutes until the cakes have risen and are just firm to the touch in the center. Remove the cakes from the oven and transfer them to a wire rack to cool.

4. For the topping, stir the crème fraîche into the melted chocolate, and let cool and thicken slightly, if necessary. Spoon or pipe onto the cupcakes. Place a raspberry on each cake before the chocolate topping sets.

Blueberry and maple syrup

· · · · · · · · ·

These cakes make good snacks for school lunches.
Freezing is not recommended because the blueberries
will become soft when defrosted.

Makes 12 standard-size cupcakes

For the cupcakes

- 9 Tbsp. (125 g, or 4½ oz.) butter, softened
- ¼ cup (60 g, or 2 oz.) superfine sugar
- 4 Tbsp. maple syrup
- 2 medium eggs
- 1 cup (125 g, or 4½ oz.) self-rising flour
- 2½ Tbsp. milk
- ¾ cup (125 g, or 4½ oz.) fresh blueberries

For the topping

- 3½ Tbsp. maple syrup

1. Preheat the oven to 375°F/190°C (gas 5).

2. To make the cupcakes, beat together the butter, sugar, and maple syrup in a bowl until the mixture is light and fluffy. Add the eggs, flour, and milk to the bowl, and beat until smooth. Stir in the blueberries.

3. Divide the mixture among the cupcake liners and bake in the center of the oven for 12 to 15 minutes until the cakes have risen and are just firm to the touch in the center. Remove the cupcakes from the oven and transfer them to a wire rack to cool.

4. For the topping, brush the maple syrup over the tops of the warm cupcakes to glaze.

Chocolate and peanut butter

. . . .

If you prefer a chunkier texture, use crunchy peanut butter instead of the creamy variety.

Makes 12 standard-size cupcakes

For the frosting

- 7 oz. (200 g) cream cheese
- ¼ cup (60 g, or 2 oz.) unsalted butter, softened
- ½ cup (125 g, or 4½ oz.) smooth peanut butter
- 1 cup (125 g, or 4½ oz.) confectioners' sugar

For the cupcakes

- 12 Chocolate cupcakes, see page 22

For the decoration

- 36 chocolate-covered peanuts

1. To make the frosting, beat the cream cheese to soften it, then add the butter and peanut butter and beat until smooth. Gradually beat in the confectioners' sugar until the frosting is light and fluffy.

2. Spread frosting over the cakes, and decorate each with 3 chocolate-covered peanuts.

Rocky road

· · · · · · · · ·

These are refrigerator cakes—no baking required!

Makes 12 standard-size cupcakes

For the chocolate cups

- 9 oz. (250 g) chocolate melting wafers, melted

For the filling

- ⅓ cup plus 1½ Tbsp. (100 mL, or 3½ fl. oz.) crème fraîche
- 7 oz. (200 g) semi-sweet chocolate, melted
- 1 cup (150 g, or 5½ oz.) digestive biscuits or graham crackers, crushed
- 2¾ cups (125 g, or 4½ oz.) mini marshmallows
- ¾ cup (100 g, 3½ oz.) walnuts, chopped

1. To make the chocolate cups, brush the inside of the cupcake liners with the melted chocolate. Place the cupcake liners in the muffin pans and let the chocolate set in the liners. Keep brushing on layers of the chocolate until all of it is used. Chill the liners for about 10 minutes. Remove the muffin pan from the refrigerator and take out the liners. Carefully peel the paper away from the chocolate cups.

2. To make the filling, stir the crème fraîche into the melted chocolate, then stir in the biscuits/graham crackers, marshmallows, and walnuts. Divide the mixture among the chocolate cups, and leave them in a cool place for at least 30 minutes until the filling has set.

Mini sticky jammy cakes

This recipe uses jam instead of sugar in the cupcakes to give them a fruity flavor.

Makes 24 mini cupcakes

For the cupcakes

° ¼ cup (60 g, or 2 oz.) butter, softened
° ¼ cup (90 g, or 3 oz.) smooth fruit jam
° ½ cup (60 g, or 2 oz.) self-rising flour
° 1 medium egg
° 1 Tbsp. milk

For the topping

° 9–12 level Tbsp. smooth fruit jam

1. Preheat the oven to 375°F/190°C (gas 5).

2. Beat together the butter and jam in a bowl until the mixture is smooth. Add the flour, egg, and milk to the bowl, and beat the mixture well.

3. Divide the mixture among the cupcake liners in a mini muffin/cupcake pan, and bake in the center of the oven for 12 to 15 minutes until the cakes have risen and are just firm to the touch in the center. Remove the cakes from the oven and transfer them to a wire rack.

4. For the topping, warm the jam and brush it thickly over the tops of the hot cupcakes, then let the cakes cool completely before serving.

Flower power

· · · · · · · ·

The colored sugar sprinkles add sparkle
to these pretty cupcakes.

Makes 12 standard-size cupcakes

For the cupcakes

○ 12 Plain cupcakes, see page 20

For the topping

○ 20 large marshmallows
   (10 pink and 10 white)
○ Pink and lilac sprinkles
○ 1 quantity of Thick glacé icing,
   see page 36
○ Few drops of pink and lilac
   liquid food coloring
○ 12 candy-coated chocolates

1. Cut each marshmallow into
   3 slices, using scissors. Cover
   one cut side of each of the pink
   marshmallows with pink sprinkles,
   and use lilac sprinkles on the
   white marshmallows.

2. Color half the glacé icing pink and
   the other half lilac. Spread the
   icing over the cupcakes. Arrange
   5 slices of marshmallow on each
   cake in a flowerlike shape, using the
   pink ones on the lilac icing and the
   lilac ones on the pink icing. Place
   a candy-coated chocolate in the
   center of each flower.

In the jungle

You can either buy ready-made animal faces, or make your own animals from sugar paste/fondant—or for speed, you can use candy, such as gummy snakes.

Makes 12 standard-size cupcakes

For the cupcakes
- 12 Quick-mix cupcakes, see page 25

For the topping
- Swiss meringue buttercream, see page 28
- Few drops of green liquid food coloring
- 3½–5 Tbsp. dried, shredded, unsweetened coconut
- 12 animals or animal faces, homemade or store bought

1. To make the topping, color the buttercream green and spread it over the cupcakes.

2. Add a few drops of green food coloring to the coconut and sprinkle it over the buttercream, pressing it down slightly. Place an animal decoration on top of each cupcake, sticking it in place with a little buttercream, if necesssary.

Butterfly cakes

Chocolate is always a favorite with children, but as an alternative use vanilla buttercream and decorate the tops with pink candy.

Makes 12 standard-size cupcakes

For the cupcakes

° 12 Plain cupcakes, see page 20

For the topping

° 1 quantity of Chocolate buttercream, see page 27
° Confectioners' sugar and cocoa for dusting
° 12 chocolate melting wafers
° Piping bag fitted with star piping tip

1. Slice the tops off the cakes and cut the tops in half.

2. Fill a piping bag fitted with a star tip with the buttercream, and pipe a swirl on top of each cupcake. Place the top cake halves in place like wings. Pipe extra buttercream between the wings. Dust the cakes with a little confectioners' sugar and cocoa, then press a chocolate melting wafer onto the top of each.

Cracklecakes

. . . .

No cooking required! Children will love to help make these,
just take care when melting the chocolate.

Makes 12 standard-size cupcakes

For the cupcakes

- 7 oz. (200 g) semi-sweet chocolate
- 2½ Tbsp. golden syrup
- 4 cups (100 g, or 3½ oz.) puffed rice cereal

For the topping

- Rainbow sprinkles

1. Melt the chocolate in a bowl, either in a microwave oven or over a pan of hot water. Stir in the golden syrup and then the puffed rice cereal.

2. Divide the mixture among the cupcake liners. Scatter the sprinkles over the tops of the cupcakes and chill to set.

Flapjacks

. . . .

Moist and chewy, these cupcakes make
a decadent breakfast treat!

Makes 12 standard-size cupcakes

For the cupcakes

- 11 Tbsp. (150 g, or 5½ oz.) butter
- ¾ cup (150 g, or 5½ oz.) light brown sugar
- 3½ Tbsp. golden syrup
- 2¾ cups (275 g, or 9½ oz.) rolled oats

For the topping

- 2 oz. (60 g) chocolate wafers, melted
- Small disposable piping bag

1. Preheat the oven to 325°F/160°C (gas 3).

2. To make the cupcakes, melt the butter, sugar, and golden syrup in a small saucepan. Stir the oats into the melted mixture and mix well.

3. Spoon the mixture into the cupcake liners and press down firmly. Bake the cupcakes in the center of the oven for 15 to 20 minutes, or until the mixture is bubbling and is a pale golden color. Remove the cakes from the oven and transfer them to a wire rack to cool.

4. For the topping, spoon the melted chocolate into a small, disposable piping bag and cut off the tip to make a small hole. Pipe random lines of chocolate over the cupcakes. Leave them in a cool place so the chocolate can set before serving.

Pretty 'n' pink

These will make any little girl's day!

Makes 24 mini cupcakes

For the cupcakes

- 24 Plain mini cupcakes, see page 20

For the topping

- 5 Tbsp. smooth strawberry jam
- 1 quantity of Swiss meringue buttercream, see page 28
- Pink food coloring
- Pink sprinkles
- Piping bag fitted with star piping tip

1. For the topping, beat the strawberry jam into the buttercream. Add a little pink food coloring to give the buttercream a deeper pink color.

2. Fill a large piping bag fitted with a star piping tip with the mixture, and pipe a swirl onto each cupcake. Scatter the sprinkles over the cupcakes.

Chocolate rosettes

. . . .

To mark extra-special occasions, cupcake style, garnish your
cupcakes with these impressive chocolate rosettes.

Makes 12 standard-size cupcakes

For the cupcakes

○ 12 Chocolate cupcakes,
  see page 22

For the topping

○ ½ quantity of Chocolate
  ganache, see page 32
○ 2 quantities of Modeling
  chocolate (page 40), one batch
  made with dark chocolate and
  one with white chocolate
○ Cocoa and confectioners'
  sugar for dusting
○ Round fluted cutters
○ Toothpicks

1. Spread a thin layer of ganache over
   the cupcakes.

2. Working on one cupcake at a
   time, roll out a small piece of dark
   modeling chocolate on a surface
   lightly dusted with cocoa, and with
   a fluted round cutter, cut out a disk
   about the same size as the top of
   the cupcake.

3. Roll around the edge with a
   toothpick to flute the disc, then
   place it on the cupcake. Roll out
   a small piece of white modeling
   chocolate on a surface lightly dusted
   with confectioners' sugar and cut
   out a smaller disk. Flute the edge
   again and stick it over the first disk.

4. Shape a small, flattened ball from
   the dark modeling chocolate,
   and press it in the center of
   the cupcake.

5. Decorate another 5 cakes in the
   same way, and then reverse the
   colors for the remaining 6 cakes.

Geometrics

· · · · · · · ·

You'll need a steady hand to pipe these designs. Be creative
and pipe each cake with a different design!

Makes 12 standard-size cupcakes

For the cupcakes

- 12 Plain cupcakes, see page 20

For the topping

- 3½–5 Tbsp. apricot jam, strained through a sieve
- 12½–18 oz. (350–500 g) white sugar paste/fondant
- Confectioners' sugar for dusting
- Royal icing, see page 34
- Liquid or paste food coloring
- Plain round cutter
- Small disposable piping bag
- Writing piping tips (optional)

1. Spread the apricot jam over the top of the cupcakes.

2. Roll out the sugar paste/fondant on a surface lightly dusted with confectioners' sugar, and use a plain, round cutter to cut out disks of icing about the same size as the tops of the cupcakes. Place the disks on the cakes, rerolling the sugar paste/fondant and cutting disks as required.

3. Color the royal icing in your choice of colors. Either use small, disposable piping bags as they are and cut off the tips to make small holes, or for more even lines, use writing piping tips (a No. 2, for example) in the bags. Pipe geometric patterns over the white sugar paste/fondant. Let the icing set before serving.

Birds' nests

· · · · · · · ·

These cupcakes can be made at any time of year,
but are particularly fun at Easter.

Makes 12 standard-size cupcakes

For the cupcakes

○ 12 Chocolate cupcakes,
see page 22

For the topping

○ Chocolate buttercream,
see page 27
○ 4–6 chocolate bars, shaved
or curled*
○ 36 sugar-coated mini
chocolate eggs

* To make chocolate shavings or
curls, draw a vegetable peeler or
grater against the smooth edges of
a chocolate bar.

1. Spread the chocolate buttercream
over the cupcakes.

2. Arrange the chocolate shavings
or curls around the edges of the
cupcakes to make the nests. Place
3 mini chocolate eggs in each nest.

GROWN-UP
FAVORITES

Caramelized banana and cinnamon

. . . .

These cupcakes have a crunchy topping—if you prefer something softer, then go for the Toffee topping on page 39.

go for the Toffee topping on page 39.

Makes 12 standard-size cupcakes

For the cupcakes

- 6 Tbsp. (90 g, or 3 oz.) butter, softened
- ½ cup (90 g, or 3 oz.) light brown sugar
- 2 medium eggs
- ¾ cup (90 g, or 3 oz.) self-rising flour
- 1 level tsp. ground cinnamon
- 1 ripe banana, mashed

For the topping

- 7 Tbsp. water
- 1 cup plus 1 Tbsp. (250 g, or 9 oz.) superfine sugar
- 2 Tbsp. (30 g, or 1 oz.) butter

1. Preheat the oven to 375°F/190°C (gas 5).

2. To make the cupcakes, beat the butter and light brown sugar together in a bowl until the mixture is light and fluffy. Add the eggs and then sift in the flour and cinnamon. Beat until the mixture is smooth, then fold in the banana.

3. Divide the mixture among the cupcake liners and bake in the center of the oven for 12 to 15 minutes until the cakes have risen and are just firm to the touch in the center. Remove the cakes from the oven and transfer them to a wire rack to cool.

4. For the topping, pour the water into a saucepan and add the superfine sugar. Place the pan over medium heat and stir until the

sugar has dissolved. Wash down any sugar crystals from the side of the pan using a damp pastry brush. Increase the heat and boil gently, without stirring, so the mixture does not crystalize, until the sugar turns to a caramel color.

5. Remove the pan from the heat and add the butter, and swirl it around until it's mixed in, but make sure you do not stir the mixture to help prevent crystalization. Pour the mixture over the cupcakes and let them set before serving.

Piña colada

It's a cocktail in a cake!

Makes 12 standard-size cupcakes

For the cupcakes

- 6 Tbsp. (90 g, or 3 oz.) butter, softened
- ½ cup (125 g, or 4½ oz.) superfine sugar
- ½ cup (125 mL, or 4¼ fl. oz.) coconut cream (from a carton)
- 2 medium eggs
- 2½ Tbsp. coconut rum
- 1¼ cups (150 g, or 5½ oz.) self-rising flour
- ⅓ cup (100 g, or 3½ oz.) candied pineapple, chopped

For the topping

- 2½ cups (300 g, or 10½ oz.) confectioners' sugar
- 1 Tbsp. coconut rum
- ⅓ cup plus 1½ Tbsp. (100 mL, or 3½ fl. oz.) coconut cream (from a carton)
- 12 pieces candied pineapple
- 12 candied or maraschino cherries
- 12 cocktail umbrellas

1. Preheat the oven to 375°F/190°C (gas 5).

2. To make the cupcakes, beat the butter and superfine sugar together until well mixed, then add the coconut cream, eggs, rum, and flour, and beat until the mixture is smooth. Stir in the candied pineapple.

3. Divide the mixture among the cupcake liners and bake in the center of the oven for 12 to 15 minutes until the cakes have risen and are just firm to the touch in the center. Remove the cakes from the oven and transfer them to a wire rack to cool.

4. For the topping, mix the confectioners' sugar and rum in a bowl, and add enough coconut cream to make a thick, glossy icing. Spread some of the icing over the top of each cupcake. Thread a piece of pineapple and a cherry onto a cocktail umbrella, and press one onto each cupcake. Let the icing set before serving.

Rum-raisin

· · · · · · · · ·

Use a dark rum for the boldest flavor in these cupcakes;
light rum tends to give a more delicate flavor.

Makes 12 standard-size cupcakes

For the cupcakes

- 9 Tbsp. (125 g, or 4½ oz.) butter, softened
- ⅔ cup (125 g, or 4½ oz.) light brown sugar
- 2 medium eggs
- 1 cup (125 g, or 4½ oz.) self-rising flour
- 2½ Tbsp. rum
- ⅔ cup (100 g, or 3½ oz.) raisins

For the topping

- 2 cups (250 g, or 9 oz.) confectioners' sugar
- 9 Tbsp. (125 g, or 4½ oz.) butter, softened
- 2½–3½ Tbsp. rum
- ½ cup (60 g, or 2 oz.) chocolate-coated raisins

1. Preheat the oven to 375°F/190°C (gas 5).

2. To make the cupcakes, beat the butter and light brown sugar in a bowl until light and fluffy. Add the eggs, flour, and rum, and beat the mixture until smooth. Stir in the raisins.

3. Divide the mixture among the cupcake liners and bake in the center of the oven for 12 to 15 minutes until the cakes have risen and are just firm to the touch in the center. Remove the cakes from the oven and transfer them to a wire rack to cool.

4. For the topping, beat together the confectioners' sugar, butter, and rum to make a smooth icing. Spread the icing over the tops of the cupcakes and top with the chocolate-coated raisins.

Very cherry

The color in the cherries will color these cupcakes pink, an effect you can take even further by topping with pink icing!

1. Preheat the oven to 375°F/190°C (gas 5).

2. To make the cupcakes, beat together the butter and superfine sugar in a bowl until the mixture is light and fluffy, then add the eggs, flour, and syrup, and beat the mixture until smooth. Stir in the cherries.

3. Divide the mixture among the cupcake liners and bake in the center of the oven for 15 to 18 minutes until the cakes have risen and are just firm to the touch in the center. Remove the cakes from the oven and transfer them to a wire rack to cool.

4. To make the topping, sift the confectioners' sugar into a bowl, and add the syrup and enough water to make a thick, spreadable icing. Color the icing pale pink, then color about 2½ tablespoons of it to a darker shade of pink and put this darker icing into the piping bag. Cut off the tip of the bag to make a small hole. Working on one cake at a time, spread the pale color over the tops of the cupcakes. Pipe over a spiral of the darker color. Repeat for all the cupcakes. Let the icing set before serving.

Makes 12 standard-size cupcakes

For the cupcakes

- 9 Tbsp. (125 g, or 4½ oz.) butter
- ⅓ cup plus 1 Tbsp. (90 g, or 3 oz.) superfine sugar
- 2 medium eggs
- 1 cup (125 g, or 4½ oz.) self-rising flour
- 1 Tbsp. syrup from a jar of maraschino cherries
- ⅓ cup (50 g, or 2 oz.) maraschino cherries, finely chopped

For the topping

- 2 cups (250 g, or 9 oz.) confectioners' sugar
- 1 Tbsp. syrup from a jar of maraschino cherries
- 1–2½ Tbsp. water
- Few drops of pink food coloring
- Small disposable piping bag

GROWN-UP FAVORITES

Irish coffee

· · · · · · · · · ·

Dusting these cupcakes with cocoa makes them
look like coffee in a cup!

Makes 12 standard-size cupcakes

For the cupcakes

- 1 Tbsp. instant coffee granules
- 1 Tbsp. boiling water
- 11 Tbsp. (150 g, or 5½ oz.) butter, softened
- ¾ cup (150 g, or 5½ oz.) light brown sugar
- 3 medium eggs
- 1¼ cups (150 g, or 5½ oz.) self-rising flour

For the topping

- 1 Tbsp. instant coffee granules
- 1 Tbsp. hot water
- 2 cups (250 g, or 9 oz.) confectioners' sugar
- 9 Tbsp. (125 g, or 4½ oz.) butter, softened
- 2½–3½ Tbsp. Irish cream liqueur
- 12 mini coffee bean chocolates
- Cocoa powder for dusting
- Piping bag fitted with star piping tip

1. Preheat the oven to 375°F/190°C (gas 5).

2. To make the cupcakes, dissolve the coffee granules in the boiling water. In a bowl, beat the butter and light brown sugar together until light and fluffy, add the eggs and flour, and pour in the coffee. Beat until the mixture is smooth.

3. Divide the mixture among the cupcake liners and bake in the center of the oven for 15 to 18 minutes until the cakes have risen and are just firm to the touch in the center. Remove the cakes from the oven and transfer them to a wire rack to cool.

4. For the topping, dissolve the coffee in the hot water in a bowl, then sift in the confectioners' sugar and add the butter. Beat until smooth, then add the Irish liqueur to taste. Fill a piping bag fitted with a star piping tip with the icing and pipe a swirl on top of each cupcake. Top each cupcake with a coffee bean chocolate and dust with a little cocoa powder.

Lavender cakes

· · · · · · · · ·

Lavender has all sorts of healthy properties—but make sure it is safe to eat and hasn't been sprayed with any chemicals.

Makes 12 standard-size cupcakes

For the cupcakes

- 2½ level Tbsp. dried lavender flowers
- ⅔ cup (125 g, or 4½ oz.) granulated sugar
- 9 Tbsp. (125 g, or 4½ oz.) butter, softened
- 2 medium eggs
- 1 cup (125 g, or 4½ oz.) self-rising flour

For the topping

- 1⅓ cups (175 g, or 6 oz.) confectioners' sugar
- 2½–3½ Tbsp. water
- Purple or lilac food coloring
- Lavender extract, optional
- 12 sprigs of fresh lavender

1. Preheat the oven to 375°F/190°C (gas 5).

2. To make the cupcakes, place the lavender flowers together with the granulated sugar in the bowl of a food processor or in a blender, and mix until the flowers are finely ground. Using a sieve, strain the sugar into a bowl and discard the flowers left in the sieve. Add the butter to the bowl and beat until fluffy. Add the eggs and flour and beat until smooth.

3. Divide the mixture among the cupcake liners and bake in the center of the oven for 12 to 15 minutes until the cakes have risen and are just firm to the touch in the center. Remove the cakes from the oven and transfer them to a wire rack to cool.

4. For the topping, sift the confectioners' sugar into a bowl and add sufficient water to give it a

thick, glossy icing. Color the icing to a pale shade of lavender with the food coloring. Add lavender extract, if using. Spread the icing over the tops of the cupcakes and press a sprig of lavender onto the top of each.

115

Cherry and coconut

For an enhanced coconut flavor, try using a coconut rum in place of the water for the glacé icing.

Makes 12 standard-size cupcakes

For the cupcakes

- 11 Tbsp. (150 g, or 5½ oz.) butter, softened
- ⅔ cup (150 g, or 5½ oz.) superfine sugar
- 3 medium eggs
- 1 cup (125 g, or 4½ oz.) self-rising flour
- ¾ cup (50 g, or 2 oz.) dried, shredded, unsweetened coconut
- 2½ Tbsp. milk
- ½ cup (100 g, or 3½ oz.) candied cherries, chopped

For the topping:

- 1 quantity of Thick glacé icing, see page 36
- 12 candied or maraschino cherries

1. Preheat the oven to 375°F/190°C (gas 5).

2. To make the cupcakes, beat together the butter and superfine sugar in a bowl. Add the eggs, flour, coconut, and milk, and beat until smooth. Stir in the cherries.

3. Divide the mixture among the cupcake liners and bake in the center of the oven for 15 to 18 minutes until the cakes have risen and are just firm to the touch in the center. Remove the cakes from the oven and transfer them to a wire rack to cool.

4. For the topping, spread the glacé icing over the cupcakes and top each with a candied or maraschino cherry.

A quick way to decorate the cupcakes is to put the icing in a large, disposable piping bag, cut off the tip, then pipe the icing onto the cupcakes.

Blueberry and cream cheese

• • • • • • • • •

Add the mint leaves just before serving so they don't wilt.

Makes 12 standard-size cupcakes

For the cupcakes
- 12 Lemon cupcakes, see page 24

For the topping
- 1 quantity of Lemon cream cheese frosting, see page 30
- 1–1¼ cup (150–175 g, or 5½–6 oz.) blueberries
- 5 Tbsp. blueberry jam, strained through a sieve
- 2½ Tbsp. water
- 12 sprigs of mint

1. Spread the frosting over the cupcakes. Arrange the blueberries on top of the cupcakes, pressing them into the frosting slightly to ensure they are secure.

2. Warm the jam with the water, either in a microwave oven or in a saucepan, then brush the glaze over the blueberries. Decorate with a sprig of mint on each cake just before serving.

Poppy seed and honey

To emphasize that these cupcakes contain honey, make bee decorations from yellow sugar paste/fondant. Use sheets of gelatin to make the wings, and paint the eyes and stripes with black food coloring.

Makes 12 standard-size cupcakes

For the cupcakes

- 11 Tbsp. (150 g, or 5½ oz.) butter, softened
- Just less than ½ cup (100 g, or 3½ oz.) superfine sugar
- 3½ Tbsp. honey
- 3 medium eggs
- 1¼ cups (150 g, or 5½ oz.) self-rising flour
- 2½ level Tbsp. poppy seeds

For the topping

- 3½ Tbsp. honey
- 3½ Tbsp. lemon juice
- Approx. 2 cups (250 g, or 9 oz.) confectioners' sugar
- Purple food coloring
- 12 bee decorations

1. Preheat the oven to 375°F/190°C (gas 5).

2. To make the cupcakes, beat together the butter, superfine sugar, and honey in a bowl until the mixture is light and fluffy. Add the eggs, flour, and poppy seeds, and beat until smooth.

3. Divide the mixture among the cupcake liners and bake in the center of the oven for 15 to 18 minutes until the cakes have risen and are just firm to the touch in the center. Remove the cupcakes from the oven and transfer them to a wire rack to cool.

4. For the topping, mix together the honey and lemon juice. Beat in enough confectioners' sugar to give a thick, glossy icing. Color the icing with the food coloring, then spread it over the cupcakes. Place a bee on top of each cupcake. Allow to set before serving.

Pistachio

· · · · · · · ·

To get a vibrant green color for the chopped nuts on the tops of the cupcakes, rub the skins off the nuts before chopping them.

Makes 12 standard-size cupcakes

For the cupcakes

- ½ cup (60 g, 2 oz.) pistachio nuts
- 1 cup (125 g, or 4½ oz.) self-rising flour
- 9 Tbsp. (125 g, or 4½ oz.) butter, softened
- ½ cup (125 g, or 4½ oz.) superfine sugar
- 2 medium eggs
- 2½ Tbsp. milk

For the topping

- 1 quantity of Cream cheese frosting, see page 30
- ¾ cup (100 g, 3½ oz.) pistachio nuts, chopped

1. Preheat the oven to 375°F/190°C (gas 5).

2. To make the cupcakes, place the pistachio nuts and flour into the bowl of a food processor, and mix until the nuts are finely ground. Alternatively, finely chop the nuts and mix them into the flour. Beat the butter and superfine sugar together in a bowl until light and fluffy, then add the flour mixture, eggs, and milk to the bowl, and beat until smooth.

3. Divide the mixture among the cupcake liners and bake in the center of the oven for 12 to 15 minutes until the cakes have risen and are just firm to the touch in the center. Remove the cakes from the oven and transfer them to a wire rack to cool.

4. For the topping, cover the cakes with the frosting and scatter the chopped pistachio nuts over them.

Saffron and raisins

Saffron is often used in savory recipes, but it's wonderful in sweet recipes, too, and it will turn these cakes bright yellow.

Makes 12 standard-size cupcakes

For the cupcakes

- Large pinch of saffron strands
- 2½ Tbsp. boiling water
- 11 Tbsp. (150 g, or 5½ oz.) butter, softened
- ⅔ cup (150 g, or 5½ oz.) superfine sugar
- 3 medium eggs
- 1¼ cups (150 g, or 5½ oz.) self-rising flour
- ⅔ cup (100 g, or 3½ oz.) golden raisins

For the topping

- ½ quantity of Thick glacé icing, see page 36
- Small disposable piping bag

1. Preheat the oven to 375°F/190°C (gas 5).

2. To make the cupcakes, place the saffron on a piece of parchment paper and place in the oven for 1 minute to dry—take care not to leave them in for too long or they will burn. Remove the saffron from the oven and crumble it into a small bowl and pour the water over it. Leave the saffron to steep for at least 20 minutes.

3. In a bowl, beat together the butter and sugar until the mixture is light and fluffy. Add the steeped saffron and liquid, eggs, and flour and beat the mixture until smooth, then stir in the golden raisins.

4. Divide the mixture among the cupcake liners and bake in the center of the oven for 12 to 15 minutes until the cakes have risen and are just firm to the touch in the center. Remove the cakes

from the oven and transfer them to a wire rack to cool.

5. For the topping, fill a small, disposable piping bag with the icing and cut off the tip of the bag to make a small hole. Pipe squiggles over the top of each cupcake and let the icing set before serving.

Marbled chocolate cakes

. . . .

If you want to be even more creative, you can make Neapolitan cakes by dividing the mixture into three and adding a pink swirl, too!

Makes 12 standard-size cupcakes

For the cupcakes

- 11 Tbsp. (150 g, or 5½ oz.) butter, softened
- ⅔ cup (150 g, or 5½ oz.) superfine sugar
- 3 medium eggs
- 1¼ cups (150 g, or 5½ oz.) self-rising flour
- 2½ level Tbsp. cocoa
- 2½ Tbsp. milk

For the topping

- 1 quantity of Chocolate ganache, see page 32
- White chocolate curls or shavings

*To make chocolate shavings or curls, draw a vegetable peeler or grater against the smooth edges of a chocolate bar.

1. Preheat the oven to 375°F/190°C (gas 5).

2. To make the cupcakes, beat the butter and sugar together in a bowl until light and fluffy, then add the eggs and flour and beat until smooth. Divide the mixture in half and place each half in separate bowls. Add the cocoa and milk to one of the bowls and beat well.

3. Spoon equal amounts of each mixture into the cupcake liners and swirl around with the tip of a knife. Bake the cakes in the center of the oven for 15 to 18 minutes, or until they have risen and are just firm to the touch in the center. Remove the cakes from the oven and transfer them to a wire rack to cool.

4. For the topping, spread some ganache over each cupcake and decorate with chocolate curls or grated chocolate.

Earl Grey

Earl Grey isn't just for drinking—it's good in cupcakes, too, and it's the perfect partner for chocolate!

Makes 12 standard-size cupcakes

For the cupcakes

- 6 Tbsp. boiling water
- 3 Earl Grey tea bags
- 11 Tbsp. (150 g, or 5½ oz.) butter, softened
- ¾ cup (150 g, or 5½ oz.) light brown sugar
- 3 medium eggs
- 1¼ cups (150 g, or 5½ oz.) self-rising flour

For the topping

- 1 quantity of Satin icing, see page 38

1. Preheat the oven to 375°F/190°C (gas 5).

2. To make the cupcakes, pour the boiling water over the tea bags and let them steep for about 5 minutes, then remove the tea bags, squeezing the liquid out of them.

3. In a bowl, beat the butter and sugar until the mixture is light and fluffy, then add the tea, eggs, and flour, and beat until smooth.

4. Divide the mixture among the cupcake liners and bake in the center of the oven for 15 to 18 minutes until the cakes have risen and are just firm to the touch in the center. Remove the cakes from the oven and transfer them to a wire rack to cool.

5. For the topping, spread the icing over the tops of the cupcakes, working quickly before it sets.

Parsnip and hazelnut

Carrot cake is really popular, but few people think of
using parsnips in a similar way.

1. Preheat the oven to 375°F/190°C (gas 5).

2. To make the cupcakes, beat together the
   butter and sugar in a bowl until light and
   fluffy. Add the eggs to the bowl and then
   sift in the flour and cinnamon. Beat the
   mixture until it is smooth, then stir in the
   parsnip and hazelnuts.

3. Divide the mixture among the cupcake
   liners and bake in the center of the oven
   for 15 to 18 minutes until the cakes have
   risen and are just firm to the touch in the
   center. Remove the cakes from the oven
   and transfer them to a wire rack to cool.

4. For the topping, spread the frosting
   over the cupcakes and top with the
   chopped hazelnuts.

Any nuts can be used
in place of the hazelnuts.
These cakes are also good with
pistachios or pecans.

*Makes 12 standard-size
cupcakes*

For the cupcakes

- 9 Tbsp. (125 g, or 4½ oz.)
  butter, softened
- ½ cup (125 g, or 4½ oz.)
  superfine sugar
- 2 medium eggs
- 1 cup plus 1 Tbsp. (125 g,
  4½ oz.) all-purpose flour
- 1 level tsp.
  ground cinnamon
- 1 small parsnip, peeled and
  finely grated
- ¾ cup (100 g, or 3½ oz.)
  hazelnuts, lightly roasted
  and chopped

For the topping

- 1 quantity of Lemon cream
  cheese frosting, see page 30
- ¾ cup (100 g, or 3½ oz.)
  hazelnuts, lightly roasted
  and chopped

GROWN-UP FAVORITES

Lemon crunch

. . . .

As these cupcakes cool, the sugar dries out to
form a delicious, crunchy crust.

Makes 12 standard-size cupcakes

For the cupcakes

- 9 Tbsp. (125 g, or 4½ oz.)
  butter, softened
- ½ cup (125 g, or 4½ oz.)
  superfine sugar
- 1 cup (125 g, or 4½ oz.)
  self-rising flour
- 2 medium eggs
- 2½ Tbsp. milk
- Finely grated zest of 1 lemon

For the topping

- 3½–5 level Tbsp.
  granulated sugar
- Juice of 1 lemon

1. Preheat the oven to 375°F/190°C
   (gas 5).

2. To make the cupcakes, beat the
   butter and superfine sugar together
   in a bowl until the mixture is light
   and fluffy. Add the flour, eggs, milk,
   and lemon zest to the bowl, and
   beat the mixture until smooth.

3. Divide the mixture among the
   cupcake liners and bake in the
   center of the oven for 12 to
   15 minutes until the cakes have
   risen and are just firm to the touch
   in the center. Remove the cakes
   from the oven and transfer them
   to a wire rack.

4. Immediately sprinkle the
   granulated sugar for the topping
   over the hot cupcakes and then
   drizzle on the lemon juice. Set the
   cakes aside to cool.

Raspberry swirls

These are like crumbly Viennese biscuits, so take care not to make too many crumbs when eating them!

Makes 12 standard-size cupcakes

For the biscuit cupcakes

- 12 Tbsp. (175 g, 6 oz.) unsalted butter, softened
- ¼ cup (60 g, or 2 oz.) superfine sugar
- 1¼ cups (150 g, or 5½ oz.) all-purpose flour
- ¼ cup (30 g, or 1 oz.) cornstarch

For the topping

- 5–6 Tbsp. raspberry jam
- Confectioners' sugar for dusting
- Piping bag fitted with large star piping tip

If you have time, chill the piped mixture in the cupcake liners before baking to help ensure it retains its shape during baking.

1. Preheat the oven to 350°F/180°C (gas 4).

2. To make the cupcakes, cream the butter and superfine sugar until light and fluffy. In a separate bowl, sift together the all-purpose flour and cornstarch, then gradually beat into the creamed mixture.

3. Fill a piping bag fitted with a large star piping tip with the creamed mixture and pipe into each cupcake liner, leaving a small hole in the center. Bake in the center of the oven for 15 to 20 minutes, until lightly golden in color. Remove the cupcakes from the oven and transfer to a wire rack to cool.

4. To finish the cakes, fill the holes in the center with the jam. Dust with confectioners' sugar.

Sticky orange and cardamom

. . . .

You can also pour custard over these cupcakes
to create a scrumptious dessert.

Makes 12 standard-size cupcakes

For the cupcakes

- 4 cardamom pods
- 11 Tbsp. (150 g, or 5½ oz.) butter, softened
- ¾ cup (150 g, or 5½ oz.) light brown sugar
- 1¼ cups (150 g, or 5½ oz.) self-rising flour
- 3 medium eggs
- Finely grated zest and juice of 1 orange

For the syrup

- Zest and juice of 1 orange
- 7 Tbsp. water
- 5 Tbsp. superfine sugar

1. Preheat the oven to 375° F/190°C (gas 5).

2. Split open the cardamom pods and discard the husks. Finely grind the seeds using a mortar and pestle.

3. To make the cupcakes, beat together the butter and light brown sugar in a bowl until it is light and fluffy. Add the flour, eggs, and orange zest and juice to the bowl, and beat until the mixture is smooth.

4. Divide the mixture among the cupcake liners and bake in the center of the oven for 15 to 20 minutes until the cakes have risen and are just firm to the touch in the center. Remove the cakes from the oven and transfer them to a wire rack.

134

5. While the cakes are baking, make the syrup. Put the zest into a small saucepan with the water and simmer for about 5 minutes until the zest has softened. Add the sugar and orange juice to the pan and simmer until the syrup has thickened slightly. Spoon some of the zest over the top of each warm cupcake and spoon over the remaining syrup. These cupcakes are good eaten warm or cold.

Rosemary and honey

· · · · · · · · ·

Be sure to choose fresh, young sprigs of rosemary
for the yummiest results.

Makes 12 standard-size cupcakes

For the cupcakes

- 11 Tbsp. (150 g, or 5½ oz.) butter, softened
- Just less than ½ cup (100 g, or 3½ oz.) superfine sugar
- 5 Tbsp. honey
- 3 medium eggs
- 1¼ cups (150 g, or 5½ oz.) self-rising flour
- 1 Tbsp. finely chopped fresh rosemary

For the topping

- ½ quantity of Thick glacé icing, see page 36
- Few drops of orange food coloring
- 12 sprigs of fresh rosemary

1. Preheat the oven to 375°F/190°C (gas 5).

2. To make the cupcakes, beat the butter, sugar, and honey together in a bowl until the mixture is light and fluffy. Add the eggs and flour to the bowl, and beat until the mixture is smooth. Then stir in the chopped rosemary.

3. Divide the mixture among the cupcake liners and bake in the center of the oven for 15 to 18 minutes until the cakes have risen and are just firm to the touch in the center. Remove the cakes from the oven and transfer them to a wire rack to cool.

4. For the topping, color the glacé icing to a pale orange color and drizzle it over the cupcakes. Press a sprig of rosemary onto the top of each cake before the icing sets.

Lime and chile

. . . .

Cupcakes with a kick! Make the chiles from red and green sugar paste/fondant to give an indication of the special ingredients in these cakes.

Makes 12 standard-size cupcakes

For the cupcakes

- 11 Tbsp. (150 g, or 5½ oz.) butter, softened
- ⅔ cup (150 g, or 5½ oz.) superfine sugar
- 3 medium eggs
- 1 cup (125 g, or 4½ oz.) self-rising flour
- 2½ level Tbsp. dried, shredded, unsweetened coconut
- Finely grated zest and juice of 1 lime
- 1 red chile, deseeded and finely chopped

For the topping

- 1 quantity of Thick glacé icing, see page 36
- Few drops of green food coloring
- 12 red chiles made from sugar paste/fondant

1. Preheat the oven to 375°F/190°C (gas 5).

2. To make the cupcakes, beat the butter and sugar together in a bowl until light and fluffy. Add the eggs, flour, coconut, lime zest and juice, and chile, and beat until smooth.

3. Divide the mixture among the cupcake liners and bake in the center of the oven for 15 to 18 minutes until the cakes have risen and are just firm to the touch in the center. Remove the cakes from the oven and transfer them to a wire rack to cool.

4. For the topping, color the icing and spread it over the cupcakes. Decorate each one with a red sugar paste/fondant chile.

CELEBRATION
CUPCAKES

Rose cupcakes

. . . .

Not only are these cupcakes decorated with rose petals, but they are scented with rosewater, too! Make sure you use rose petals that have not been sprayed with any harmful chemicals.

Makes 12 standard-size cupcakes

For the cupcakes

- 11 Tbsp. (150 g, or 5½ oz.) butter, softened
- ⅔ cup (150 g, or 5½ oz.) superfine sugar
- 3 medium eggs
- 1¼ cups (150 g, or 5½ oz.) self-rising flour
- 2½ Tbsp. rosewater

For the topping

- 12 rose petals
- 1 egg white, lightly beaten
- 5–7 Tbsp. superfine sugar
- 2¾ cups (350 g, or 12½ oz.) confectioners' sugar
- 3½–5 Tbsp. rosewater
- Pink food coloring

1. Preheat the oven to 375°F/190°C (gas 5).

2. To make the cupcakes, beat together the butter and sugar in a bowl until light and fluffy. Add the eggs, flour, and rosewater to the bowl and beat until the mixture is smooth. Divide the mixture among the cupcake liners and bake in the center of the oven for 15 to 18 minutes until the cakes have risen and are just firm to the touch in the center. Remove the cakes from the oven and transfer them to a wire rack to cool.

3. To crystalize the rose petals, brush them with egg white and lightly sprinkle with superfine sugar. Place them on a sheet of parchment paper and set them aside to dry.

4. To make the icing, sift the confectioners' sugar into a bowl and add sufficient rosewater to make a thick, glossy icing. Color the icing a pale pink. Spread the icing on top of the cupcakes and place a crystalized rose petal on each.

Spider cakes

· · · · · · · · ·

These cakes are ideal for a Halloween party! Look for spider-shaped candy as an alternative to piping the designs.

Makes 12 standard-size cupcakes

For the cupcakes

- 12 Quick-mix cupcakes, see page 25

For the topping

- 3½–5 Tbsp. apricot jam, strained through a sieve
- 9 oz. (250 g) orange sugar paste/fondant
- Confectioners' sugar for dusting
- 4½ oz. (125 g) chocolate melting wafers, melted
- Round fluted cutter
- Small disposable piping bag

1. If necessary, cut the tops off the cupcakes to level them. Spread the apricot jam over the tops of the cakes.

2. Roll out the orange sugar paste/fondant on a surface lightly dusted with confectioners' sugar, and use a fluted, round cutter to cut out disks of sugar paste/fondant the same size as the tops of the cupcakes. Reroll the sugar paste/fondant as necessary to cover all the cupcakes.

3. Fill a small, disposable piping bag with the melted chocolate and pipe a spider design on half the cupcakes, and spiderwebs on the other half. Let the chocolate set before serving.

Merry cupcakes

· · · · · · · ·

Dried cranberries add a seasonal touch to these spiced cakes, but currants or raisins may be substituted if dried cranberries are unavailable.

Makes 12 standard-size cupcakes

For the cupcakes

- 9 Tbsp. (125 g, or 4½ oz.) butter
- ½ cup (125 g, or 4½ oz.) superfine sugar
- 2 medium eggs
- 2½ Tbsp. milk
- 1 cup (125 g, or 4½ oz.) self-rising flour
- 1 level tsp. ground allspice
- ¾ cup (100 g, or 3½ oz.) dried cranberries

For the decoration

- 9 oz. (250 g) white sugar paste/fondant
- Green and red paste food coloring
- Confectioners' sugar for dusting
- 1 quantity of Royal icing, see page 34
- 1 Tbsp. glycerine
- Holly leaf cutter

1. Preheat the oven to 375°F/190°C (gas 5).

2. To make the cupcakes, beat together the butter and superfine sugar in a bowl until light and fluffy. Add the eggs and milk to the bowl, and then sift in the flour and allspice, beating the mixture until it is smooth. Stir in the cranberries. Divide the mixture among the cupcake liners and bake in the center of the oven for 15 to 18 minutes until the cakes have risen and are just firm to the touch in the center. Remove the cakes from the oven and transfer them to a wire rack to cool.

3. To make the decoration, color half the sugar paste/fondant green and the rest red. Roll out the green paste on a surface lightly dusted with confectioners' sugar. Cut out the leaf shapes using a holly-leaf cutter. Use the back of a small knife to mark veining on the leaves. Make 12 leaves. Roll the red sugar

paste/fondant into small balls to make 36 holly berries.

4. Stir the glycerine into the royal icing, then spread it onto the cupcakes, using a small palette knife to make peaks to look like snow. Decorate each cupcake with a holly leaf and three berries. Let the royal icing set before serving.

Gold chocolate

Pure gold leaf is used on these cakes to achieve
the height of cupcake indulgence!

*Makes 12 standard-size
cupcakes*

For the cupcakes

○ 7 Tbsp. (100 g, or
  3½ oz.) butter, softened
○ Just less than ½ cup
  (100 g, or 3½ oz.)
  superfine sugar
○ 3½ oz. (100 g) chocolate,
  melted
○ Few drops of vanilla
  extract
○ 2 medium eggs, separated
○ ¾ cup plus 1 Tbsp.
  (100 g, or 3½ oz.) all-
  purpose flour

For the topping

○ 5–7 level Tbsp. apricot
  glaze or jam, strained
  through a sieve
○ 1 quantity of Chocolate
  ganache, see page 32, at
  pouring consistency
○ Edible gold leaf transfer

1. Preheat the oven to 325°F/160°C (gas 3).

2. To make the cupcakes, beat together
   the butter and sugar in a bowl until the
   mixture is light and fluffy. Beat in the
   chocolate and vanilla extract, then beat in
   the yolks one at a time. Fold in the flour.

3. In a separate bowl, whisk the egg
   whites until stiff and fold them into the
   chocolate mixture.

4. Divide the mixture among the cupcake
   liners and bake in the center of the oven
   for 15 to 20 minutes until the cakes have
   risen and are just firm to the touch in the
   center. Remove the cakes from the oven
   and transfer them to a wire rack to cool.
   Cut off the tops of the cupcakes to level
   them, if necessary.

5. Warm the apricot glaze and brush it
   over the tops of the cakes. Pour the
   ganache over the cupcakes, then leave
   them in a cool place to set. Press a small
   fleck of gold leaf on top of each cake
   before serving.

Daisy fresh

• • • • • • • •

Decorate these with bright colors for a child's birthday party,
or all white for a christening or wedding.

Makes 24 mini cupcakes

For the cupcakes

○ 24 Plain mini cupcakes, see
  page 20

For the topping

○ 4½–6 oz. (125–175 g)
  white sugar paste/fondant
○ Confectioners' sugar for
  dusting
○ Paste food coloring in
  assorted colors
○ 1 quantity of Royal icing,
  see page 34
○ 1 Tbsp. glycerine
○ Daisy cutter
○ Egg cartons or cupped pieces
  of foil
○ Small disposable piping bag

1. To make the daisies, divide the
   sugar paste/fondant into several
   pieces and color each piece a
   different color. Roll out one color
   on a surface lightly dusted with
   confectioners' sugar, and use a daisy
   cutter to cut out shapes. To dry,
   place the flowers in a curve-shaped
   container, such as an egg carton, or
   use a cupped piece of foil. Color a
   small amount of royal icing yellow,
   and fill a piping bag. Cut off the
   tip of the bag and pipe dots in the
   centers of the flowers.

2. Stir the glycerine into the
   remaining royal icing and color it
   in different shades to coordinate
   with the flowers. Add sufficient
   water to the icing so that it flows
   smoothly but is still firm enough
   to hold its shape. Spread the icing
   over the tops of the cupcakes and
   stick a flower on top of each. Let
   the icing set before serving.

True love

● ● ● ● ● ● ● ●

To save time, you can use ready-made sugar heart decorations, which are available from stores where cake decorating supplies are sold.

Makes 12 standard-size cupcakes

For the cupcakes

° 12 Plain cupcakes, see page 20

For the topping

° 4½ oz. (125 g) sugar paste/fondant colored red
° Confectioners' sugar for dusting
° 3 oz. (90 g) sugar paste/fondant colored pink
° Swiss meringue buttercream, see page 28
° 2 different sizes of heart cutters
° Cutting board lined with parchment paper
° Piping bag fitted with large star piping tip

1. To make the hearts, roll out the red sugar paste/fondant on a surface lightly dusted with confectioners' sugar. Use a large heart cutter to cut out 12 hearts, rerolling the sugar paste/fondant as necessary. Place the hearts on a cutting board lined with parchment paper so they don't stick to the work surface. Roll out the pink sugar paste/fondant and cut out 12 smaller hearts. Brush a little water onto the backs of each pink heart and stick one in the center of each red heart. Let the hearts dry, preferably overnight.

2. Fill a piping bag fitted with a large star piping tip with the buttercream. Pipe a swirl onto the top of each cupcake, and place a heart on each.

Spring garden

· · · · · · · · ·

The flower decorations may be made several days or even weeks in advance and stored in a cardboard box with parchment paper between layers. Store any extra flowers this way; as long as they are kept dry, they will last for several months.

Makes 12 standard-size cupcakes

For the cupcakes

° 12 Lemon cupcakes, see page 24

For the topping

° 2 quantities of Royal icing, see page 34
° Liquid or paste food coloring
° 1 Tbsp. glycerine
° Disposable piping bags
° Drop flower piping tips
° Tray lined with parchment paper
° Leaf piping tip

1. Color the royal icing as required: either make the flowers all the same color or make them in assorted colors. Cut the tip off a piping bag and insert a drop flower piping tip. Fill the bag with royal icing and pipe flowers onto a parchment paper-lined tray. Do this by holding the piping bag so that the tip touches the parchment paper. Squeeze the bag and twist it slightly while squeezing the icing, then stop squeezing and lift the tip away from the flower.

2. Let the flowers dry. Pipe the centers of the flower in a contrasting color of royal icing, using a piping bag with the tip cut off to make a small hole. Color some royal icing green and pipe leaves onto the parchment paper. Allow the flowers and leaves to dry, then gently peel them off the parchment paper.

3. Stir the glycerine into the remaining royal icing and color as desired. Add a little water to the icing so it looks glossy and is thick enough to spread but not too runny. Spread the icing over the cupcakes, and place the flowers and leaves on top.

Fishy wishy

· · · · · · · · ·

A mixture of fish candles and chocolate shells provide the underwater theme to these cakes—or you could use your imagination and model your own fish from sugar paste/fondant!

Makes 12 standard-size cupcakes

For the cupcakes

○ 12 Plain cupcakes, see page 20

For the shells

○ Candy colors (oil-based food coloring), various colors
○ 4½ oz. (125 g) white chocolate melting wafers

For the topping

○ 1 quantity of Swiss meringue buttercream, see page 28
○ Blue and green food coloring
○ Fish candles
○ Seashell molds

1. To make the shells, smear some of the food coloring over the inside surface of the seashell molds. Melt the white chocolate melting wafers in a bowl in a microwave or over a pan of hot water. Spoon the melted mixture into the molds. Tap the molds to knock out any air bubbles, then place them in the refrigerator until the mixture has set. Gently tip the chocolates out of the mold.

2. Color the buttercream for the topping using the blue and green food coloring, but without mixing it in properly so that it looks marbled. Spread the buttercream over the cupcakes, and place the candles onto some and the chocolate shells onto the rest.

Chocolate roses

. . . .

Roses lend a certain elegance to any occasion. For more romantic cakes, make the roses from red modeling chocolate.

Makes 12 standard-size cupcakes

For the cupcakes

- 11 Tbsp. (150 g, or 5½ oz.) butter, softened
- ⅔ cup (150 g, or 5½ oz.) superfine sugar
- 3 medium eggs
- Finely grated zest and 2½ Tbsp. juice from 1 orange
- 1 cup (125 g, or 4½ oz.) self-rising flour
- 2½ level Tbsp. cocoa

For the topping

- 1 quantity of Modeling chocolate, see page 40
- Cocoa for dusting
- 3½ Tbsp. crème fraîche
- 250 g (9 oz) white chocolate melting wafers, melted and colored with orange candy color
- Rose leaf cutters

1. Preheat the oven to 375°F/190°C (gas 5).

2. To make the cupcakes, beat together the butter and sugar in a bowl until light and fluffy. Add the eggs and orange zest and juice to the bowl, and sift in the flour and cocoa, beating until the mixture is smooth. Divide the mixture among the cupcake liners and bake in the center of the oven for 12 to 15 minutes until the cakes have risen and are just firm to the touch in the center. Remove the cakes from the oven and transfer them to a wire rack to cool.

3. For the rose leaves, roll out the modeling chocolate, dusting the surface with cocoa, and cut out 36 leaves. Mark veining on the leaves using the back of a knife, and twist the leaves slightly. Make the roses by shaping a cone of the modeling chocolate, then make petals from flattened teardrop shapes and wrap them around the cone. Add about

six petals to each rose, then cut off the rose to make a flat base.

4. To make the topping, stir the crème fraîche into the melted chocolate, and if necessary let it cool slightly until it is of a spreadable consistency. Spread the orange topping over the cupcakes and then place 3 leaves and a flower on top of each cupcake.

Simply white

Using a textured rolling pin adds a pattern to the tops of these cupcakes, but if you don't have one, you can emboss the tops of the cakes using the handle of a fancy spoon.

Makes 12 standard-size cupcakes

For the cupcakes

○ 12 Plain cupcakes, see page 20

For the topping

○ 3½–5 Tbsp. apricot glaze or jam, strained through a sieve
○ 12½ oz. (350 g) white sugar paste/fondant
○ Confectioners' sugar for dusting
○ Edible white luster dust
○ 2½–3½ Tbsp. strong, clear alcohol (alcohol-based rosewater, for example)
○ Round fluted cutter
○ Blossom flower cutter
○ Textured rolling pin

1. Spread the apricot glaze over the tops of the cupcakes.

2. Roll out the sugar paste/fondant on a surface lightly dusted with confectioners' sugar. Roll over the surface of the sugar paste/fondant with a textured rolling pin, pressing firmly to ensure the design shows. Use a round, fluted cutter to cut out disks to cover the tops of the cakes.

3. Reroll the trimmings and cut out 36 blossom flowers using a flower blossom cutter. Roll a small ball of sugar paste/fondant for the center of each flower. Paint a little water into the center and place the ball of sugar paste/fondant in place. Mix the luster dust with the alcohol and paint over the embossed design on the cupcakes, as well as the centers of the flowers. Brush a little water on the backs of the flowers, and place 3 onto each cupcake while the sugar paste/fondant is still soft.

Starry, snowy night

The stars may be made several days in advance to ensure they are thoroughly dried out—then it takes no time at all to decorate these cakes.

Makes 12 standard-size cupcakes

For the cupcakes

° 12 Lemon cupcakes, see page 24

For the decoration

° 9 oz. (250 g) white sugar paste/fondant
° Confectioners' sugar for dusting
° Edible silver luster dust
° 2½–3½ Tbsp. strong, clear alcohol (alcohol-based rosewater, for example)
° Silver balls
° 1 Tbsp. glycerine
° 1 quantity of Royal icing, see page 34
° Star cutters
° Cutting board lined with parchment paper

1. Roll out the white sugar paste/ fondant on a surface lightly dusted with confectioners' sugar, and cut out star shapes: 12 large stars with the center cut out and 36 small stars. Let the stars dry on a board lined with parchment paper. Mix some silver luster dust with the alcohol, and paint the stars. Place the stars on a sheet of parchment paper to dry.

2. Stir the glycerine into the royal icing, and spread it over the tops of the cupcakes using a small palette knife to form peaks. While the royal icing is still soft, place 1 large and 3 small stars onto the tops of the cupcakes, along with a few silver balls. Let the icing set before serving.

1 today!

. . . .

These cakes may be adapted to any occasion when decorated with
the appropriate numbers and candy or candles. For example,
use champagne bottle candles for a 21st birthday.

Makes 12 standard-size cupcakes

For the cupcakes

o 12 Plain cupcakes, see page 20

For the topping

o 4½ oz. (125 g) yellow sugar
  paste/fondant
o Confectioners' sugar for
  dusting
o Blue food coloring
o 1 quantity of Swiss meringue
  buttercream, see page 28
o Multicolored fish sprinkles
o Number cutters
o Parchment paper
o 6 duck candles

1. To make the numbers, roll out
   the sugar paste/fondant on
   a surface lightly dusted with
   confectioners' sugar. Cut out at
   least 6 numbers using number
   cutters, and let them dry on a
   sheet of parchment paper. Turn
   them over after 4 to 6 hours, and
   leave them overnight so they
   dry completely.

2. To make the topping, color the
   buttercream blue, and spread it
   over the tops of the cupcakes. Place
   numbers into the buttercream
   on half the cupcakes and scatter
   the fish sprinkles. Decorate
   the remaining cakes with the
   duck candy.

Chocolate love

· · · · · · · ·

To make these cakes even more special, you can brush
the hearts with edible gold luster dust.

Makes 12 standard-size cupcakes

For the cupcakes

○ 12 Chocolate cupcakes,
see page 22

For the topping

○ 3½ oz. (100 g) white chocolate
melting wafers, melted
○ 1 quantity of Chocolate
ganache, see page 32
○ Small disposable piping bag
○ Tray lined with
parchment paper

1. To make the hearts, fill a small
piping bag with the melted
chocolate, and cut off the tip to
make a small hole. You will need 24
heart shapes, but pipe a few extra
to allow for any breakages. Place
the hearts on a tray lined with
parchment paper, and leave them
in a cool place to set, then carefully
slide a palette knife under them to
release them from the paper.

2. Spread the ganache over the
cupcakes, and place 2 hearts on
the top of each cake.

166

Mini birthday bows

. . . .

The bows may be made several days in advance so they are ready to place on the cupcakes. The sugar paste/fondant quantity below is enough to make a bow for each cupcake.

Makes 24 mini cupcakes

For the cupcakes

- 24 Plain mini cupcakes, see page 20

For the topping:

- 18 oz. (500 g) white sugar paste/fondant
- Paste food coloring in pink and blue
- Confectioners' sugar for dusting
- 1 quantity of Thick glacé icing, see page 36
- 2 large disposable piping bags

1. Divide the sugar paste/fondant into two equal portions, and use the paste color to color one half pink and the other blue. Working with one color at a time, roll it out on a surface lightly dusted with confectioners' sugar and cut out 2 long, narrow strips. Fold the ends of the strips over to make loops, then crisscross these 2 strips over each other to give a bow shape. Brush a little water where they join and press the pieces together. Wrap a strip around the center as the knot of the bow. Cut off the ends to the right length to finish the bow. Make 12 bows of each color.

2. Color half the glacé icing pink and the other half blue. Fill 2 large piping bags with each color and cut the tips off. Pipe pink icing on half the cakes and blue on the other half. Stick bows on half the cakes and leave the remaining cakes plain.

SPECIAL
DIETS

Chocolate surprise

Keep people guessing what the secret ingredient
is in these cupcakes!

Makes 12 standard-size cupcakes

For the cupcakes

- ¾ lb. (350 g, or 12½ oz.) potatoes, peeled
- 3 Tbsp. (45 g, or 1½ oz.) butter
- ⅔ cup (100 g, or 3½ oz.) chocolate, coarsely chopped
- 3 medium eggs, separated
- ¼ cup (60 g, or 2 oz.) superfine sugar

For the topping

- ⅓ cup plus 1½ Tbsp. (100 mL, or 3½ fl. oz.) crème fraîche
- 7 oz. (200 g) chocolate, melted
- 2–3 chocolate bars, curled or shaved

*To make chocolate shavings or curls, draw a vegetable peeler or grater against the smooth edges of a chocolate bar.

1. Preheat the oven to 375°F/190°C (gas 5).

2. Cut the potatoes into chunks, place in a large saucepan, and cover with water. Bring to a boil, then simmer for 15 to 20 minutes or until tender. Remove the pan from the heat and drain the potatoes. Return them to the pan, add the butter, and mash well. Add the chocolate and stir until it has melted. Set aside to cool.

3. In a bowl, whisk the egg yolks and sugar together, preferably using an electric mixer, until the mixture is thick and creamy and leaves a trail when the beaters are lifted. Fold into the mashed potato. In a separate bowl, whisk the egg whites until stiff, then fold into the chocolate potato mixture.

4. Divide the mixture among the cupcake liners and bake in the center of the oven for 15 to

SPECIAL DIETS

20 minutes until the cakes have risen and are just firm to the touch in the center. Remove the cakes from the oven and transfer them to a wire rack to cool.

5. For the topping, stir the crème fraîche into the chocolate, then spread some onto each cupcake. Top each cake with chocolate curls or shavings.

Date and banana

Use soft, juicy dates, such as Medjool dates when they are available, for the best flavor.

Makes 12 standard-size cupcakes

For the cupcakes

- 1 cup (125 g, or 4½ oz.) gluten-free flour
- 2 Tbsp. (30 g, or 1 oz.) light brown sugar
- ¾ cup plus 1 Tbsp. (125 g, or 4½ oz.) dates, pitted and chopped
- 1 level tsp. gluten-free baking powder
- 2 medium eggs
- 5 Tbsp. vegetable oil
- 1 ripe banana, peeled and mashed

For the topping

- Cream cheese frosting, see page 30

1. Preheat the oven to 400°F/200°C (gas 6).

2. To make the cupcakes, pour the flour and sugar together in a bowl, then stir in the dates and baking powder.

3. In a separate bowl, lightly whisk the eggs and oil together, and stir in the mashed banana. Stir this mixture into the dry mixture.

4. Divide the mixture among the cupcake liners and bake in the center of the oven for 15 to 20 minutes until the cakes have risen and are just firm to the touch in the center. Remove the cakes from the oven and transfer them to a wire rack to cool.

5. For the topping, spread the cream cheese frosting over the cupcakes and texture the surface with a fork.

SPECIAL DIETS

Currant cupcakes

· · · · · · · ·

The vinegar in this recipe evaporates during cooking,
so the cakes don't taste at all acidic!

Makes 12 standard-size cupcakes

For the cupcakes

- 1¼ cup (150 g, or 5½ oz.) all-purpose flour
- 4 Tbsp. (60 g, or 2 oz.) butter
- 1⅓ cups (200 g, or 7 oz.) currants
- 1 cup (75 g, or 2½ oz.) chopped, candied citrus peel
- ⅔ cup (125 g, or 4½ oz.) light brown sugar
- ⅓ cup plus 1½ Tbsp. (100 mL, or 3½ fl. oz.) milk
- ½ level tsp. baking soda
- 2 Tbsp. malt vinegar

For the topping

- ½ quantity of Thick glacé icing, see page 36

1. Preheat the oven to 325°F/160°C (gas 3).

2. Sift the flour into a bowl and rub in the butter, then stir in the currants, citrus peel, and sugar. Warm the milk gently in a pan, then sprinkle with the baking soda and stir in the vinegar. While it's foaming, stir it into the flour and fruit mixture.

3. Divide the mixture among the cupcake liners and bake in the center of the oven for 20 to 25 minutes until the cupcakes have risen and are just firm to the touch in the center. Remove the cakes from the oven and transfer them to a wire rack to cool.

4. For the topping, drizzle some glacé icing over each cupcake and let the icing set before serving.

REDUCED FAT

Chocolate and prune

A prune purée is used in place of butter in this recipe. The prunes also add sweetness without adding extra sugar.

Makes 12 standard-size cupcakes

For the cupcakes

- 2 cups (250 g, or 9 oz.) pitted prunes
- 1¼ cups (300 mL, or 10 fl. oz.) boiling water
- 1 tsp. vanilla extract
- ¾ cup (100 g, or 3½ oz.) self-rising flour
- 2 oz. (50 g) chocolate, melted
- 2 medium egg whites

For the topping:

- Confectioners' sugar for dusting

1. Preheat the oven to 350°F/180°C (gas 4).

2. Place the prunes in a bowl and pour the boiling water over them. Let them soak for at least 30 minutes, then pulse the prunes and water in a food processor or blender until smooth.

3. Put the prune mixture in a bowl, add the vanilla extract and flour, then stir in the melted chocolate.

4. In a separate bowl, whisk the egg whites until they are stiff and fold them into the prune mixture.

5. Divide the mixture among the cupcake liners, and bake in the center of the oven for 20 to 25 minutes until the cakes have risen and are just firm to the touch in the center. Remove the cakes from the oven and transfer them to a wire rack to cool.

6. For the topping, dust the cupcakes with confectioners' sugar sifted through a fine strainer.

SPECIAL DIETS

Honey and bran

These sticky-topped cakes make a good
weekend breakfast treat.

Makes 12 standard-size cupcakes

For the cupcakes

- 1 cup (125 g, or 4½ oz.)
  self-rising flour
- 1⅔ cups (90 g, or 3 oz.)
  wheat bran
- 1 level tsp. baking powder
- 5 Tbsp. soy milk
- 7 Tbsp. honey
- 2 medium eggs
- 5 Tbsp. vegetable oil

For the topping

- 5 Tbsp. honey
- Juice and zest of 1 lemon
- Approx. 1⅔ cups (200 g,
  or 7 oz.) confectioners' sugar

1. Preheat the oven to 400°F/200°C
   (gas 6).

2. To make the cupcakes, mix together
   the flour, bran, and baking powder in
   a bowl.

3. In a separate bowl, lightly beat together
   the soy milk, honey, egg, and oil, then
   stir into the dry ingredients. Stir lightly
   and don't overmix or the cupcakes will
   be tough.

4. Divide the mixture among the cupcake
   liners and bake in the center of the
   oven for 12 to 15 minutes until the
   cakes have risen and are just firm to the
   touch in the center. Remove the cakes
   from the oven and transfer them to a
   wire rack.

5. For the topping, mix together the honey
   and the lemon juice, and beat in enough
   confectioners' sugar to make a thick,
   glossy icing. Spread the icing over the
   tops of the cupcakes and scatter a few
   strands of the lemon zest over each.
   Let the icing set before serving.

Date and apple

The demerara sugar on the tops of these cupcakes
gives them a pleasant crunch.

Makes 12 standard-size cupcakes

For the cupcakes

- 1 cup (125 g, or 4½ oz.) gluten-free flour
- 2½ level tsp. gluten-free baking powder
- 1 level tsp. ground cinnamon
- 6 Tbsp. (90 g, or 3 oz.) butter, softened
- 5 Tbsp. light brown sugar
- 1 apple, cored and grated
- 2 medium eggs
- 2½ Tbsp. milk
- 1 cup (150 g, or 5½ oz.) dates, pitted and finely chopped

For the topping

- 3½–5 level Tbsp. demerara sugar

1. Preheat the oven to 350°F/180°C (gas 4).

2. To make the cupcakes, sift the flour, baking powder, and cinnamon into a bowl. Add the butter, light brown sugar, apple, eggs, and milk, and beat until smooth. Stir in the dates. Spoon the mixture into the cupcake liners and level the surface.

3. For the topping, sprinkle the demerara sugar over the cupcakes. Bake in the center of the oven for 15 to 20 minutes until the cakes have risen and are just firm to the touch in the center. Remove the cakes from the oven and transfer them to a wire rack to cool.

SPECIAL DIETS

Blueberry and vanilla

Blueberries help to sweeten these cupcakes while the hazlenuts and vanilla add wonderful flavor.

1. Preheat the oven to 350°F/180°C (gas 4).

2. To make the cupcakes, place the butter, fruit sugar, flour, eggs, and vanilla extract in a bowl, and beat until smooth. Stir in the blueberries.

3. Divide the mixture among the cupcake liners, and scatter the hazlenuts over the tops. Bake in the center of the oven for 12 to 15 minutes until the cakes have risen and are a light golden color. Take care not to overcook them or the blueberries will break down and get mushy. Remove the cakes from the oven and transfer them to a wire rack.

Makes 12 standard-size cupcakes

For the cupcakes

- 7 Tbsp. (100 g, or 3 ½ oz) butter, softened
- ¼ cup (50 g, or 2 oz.) fruit sugar (fructose)
- ¾ cup (100 g, or 3 ½ oz.) self-rising flour
- 2 medium eggs
- Few drops of vanilla extract
- 1 cup (100 g, or 3 ½ oz.) blueberries
- ¼ cup (30 g, or 1 oz.) hazelnuts, roughly chopped

Freezing these cupcakes is not recommended because the blueberries will get soft once they have thawed.

SPECIAL DIETS

Ginger polenta

This doesn't look like a polenta recipe, as the dark brown sugar disguises the yellow color of the polenta.

Makes 12 standard-size cupcakes

For the cupcakes

- 9 Tbsp. (125 g, or 4½ oz.) butter, softened
- ⅔ cup (125 g, or 4½ oz.) dark brown sugar
- 1 Tbsp. ground ginger
- Pinch salt
- 3 medium eggs
- ¾ cup (125 g, or 4½ oz.) fine polenta
- ¾ cup (100 g, or 3½ oz.) ground almonds
- 1 level tsp. gluten-free baking powder
- 5 Tbsp. milk

For the topping

- 6 pieces stem ginger in syrup
- 2½–3½ Tbsp. ginger syrup (from stem ginger jar)

1. Preheat the oven to 325°F/160°C (gas 3).

2. To make the cupcakes, beat the butter, dark brown sugar, ground ginger, and salt together until light and fluffy, then beat in the eggs. Fold in the polenta, along with the almonds and baking powder. Spoon the mixture into the cupcake liners, leveling the surface of each. Bake in the center of the oven for 15 to 20 minutes until the cakes have risen and are just firm to the touch in the center. Remove the cakes from the oven and transfer them to a wire rack to cool.

3. For the topping, cut the stem ginger into long strips and scatter them over the cupcakes, and then spoon some of the syrup over the tops.

Halloween webs

· · · · · · · · ·

These cobwebby cupcakes look best in contrasting colors.
To save time, use just two colors for each cake.

Makes 12 standard-size cupcakes

For the cupcakes

- 9 Tbsp. (125 g, or 4½ oz.) butter, softened
- ½ cup (125 g, or 4½ oz.) superfine sugar
- 2 medium eggs
- 2½ Tbsp. milk
- 1 cup (125 g, or 4½ oz.) gluten-free flour
- 1 level tsp. gluten-free baking powder

For the topping

- 1 quantity of Thick glacé icing, see page 36
- 4 liquid or paste food colors
- 4 disposable piping bags
- Toothpick

1. Preheat the oven to 375°F/190°C (gas 5).

2. To make the cupcakes, beat the butter and sugar together in a bowl until the mixture is light and fluffy. Add the eggs and milk, then sift in the flour and baking powder. Beat the mixture until smooth. Divide the mixture among the cupcake liners and bake in the center of the oven for 12 to 15 minutes until the cakes have risen and are just firm to the touch in the center. Remove the cakes from the oven and transfer them to a wire rack to cool.

3. For the topping, divide the glacé icing into 4 equal portions, and take out 2½ tablespoons from each portion. Color each main portion in different colors and each smaller portion, which will be used for the webs, in contrasting colors. Working on one cupcake at a time, spread over the main color. Place the contrasting icing in a piping bag, cut off the tip, and pipe a spiral over the icing. Pull a toothpick through the spiral from the center out to give a web effect. Decorate 3 cupcakes with each color combination.

Substitutions

· · · · · · · · ·

Some recipes call for ingredients that you probably don't have at home and may find difficult to source if you don't live in a major city or have easy access to the Internet. In such cases, substitutions can be made. The following are only suggestions.

Original	Substitute
crème fraiche	sour cream. Alternatively, use a whisked 1:1 mixture of sour cream and heavy whipping cream, or a full fat Greek yogurt
berry conserve	use the corresponding jam (strawberry jam in place of strawberry conserve, for instance)
kirsch	Kirsch (*kirschwasser*) is a Black Forest brandy made from morello cherries, and is not sweet. There is no real substitute, but in a pinch, use fruit brandy, sour cherry juice, or cognac
golden syrup	Golden syrup is a distinctly British pastry ingredient for which there is no real substitute. You may be able to find it at a large supermarket or online. If substituting, use a 2:1 mixture of light corn syrup and molasses, or, in a pinch, maple syrup or agave nectar, though the taste won't be the same
digestive biscuits	graham crackers
stem ginger	crystallized ginger

Acknowledgments

The author would like to thank the following companies for supplying ingredients and equipment for the testing of recipes and photography for this book. All of these companies offer online ordering:

Beryls
5520 Hempstead Way
Springfield, VA 22151
USA
www.beryls.com

Knightsbridge PME
Cake Decoration
Unit 23
Riverwalk Road
Enfield EN3 7QN
England
www.pmecake.co.uk

Squires Kitchen Shop
3 Waverley Lane
Farnham
Surrey GU9 8BB
England
www.squires-shop.com

Index

Shutterstock photos: Iryna Denysova (orange zest, page 135), EasterBunny
(baking utensils, pages 6–7), everydayplus (baking ingredients, pages 18–19),
freesoulproduction (cupcake icon, page 3), Hurst Photo (butter, page 12), istetiana
(strawberries and cream cupcakes, pages 42–43), KnottoSS (birthday cupcakes,
pages 140–41), Nattika (cinnamon, page 107), Tejal Pandya (saffron, page 125),
RJ Design (bluberry cupcakes, pages 170–71), simonidadj (cupcakes, pages 72–73),
soeka (chocolate cupcakes, pages 104–105).